The Army of the Swabian League 1525

Douglas Miller

Helion & Company

Helion & Company Limited
Unit 8 Amherst Business Centre
Budbrooke Road
Warwick
CV34 5WE
England
Tel. 01926 499 619
Email: info@helion.co.uk
Website: www.helion.co.uk
Twitter: @helionbooks

Published by Helion & Company 2019
Designed and typeset by Mach 3 Solutions Ltd (www.mach3solutions.co.uk)
Cover designed by Paul Hewitt, Battlefield Design (www.battlefield-design.co.uk)

ISBN: 978-1-912866-51-9

British Library Cataloguing-in-Publication Data.
A catalogue record for this book is available from the British Library.

Contents

List of Illustrations

Part 1

Part 2

Maps

Tables

Boxes

Chronology

1524

June 23	Stühlingen Uprising
August 24	Stühlingen rebels ally with the town of Waldshut. Georg Truchsess von Waldburg receives his commission from Archduke Ferdinand of Austria
October 2	Hegau uprising – Stühlingen band marches through the upper Black Forest
Mid October	Open rebellion in Klettgau Georg Truchsess von Waldburg appointed commander of the Austrian troops mobilised to quell the early uprisings
November	(middle) Revolt spills over into Breisgau
December 14	Black Forest peasants suffer a defeat at Donaueschingen
24	Creation of the Baltringen band

1525

January 23	Rebellion in the Allgäu – peasant assembly at Leubas
30	The Swabian League strikes an agreement with the peasants of Villingen
February 5	Ongoing meetings of the League Council in Ulm
11	The Swabian League requests the requests first third contingent
15	Georg von Waldburg appointed supreme commander of the League army Declaration of War by the League.
16/17	Letter of Grievances submitted by the Baltringen band to the Swabian League
18	Second third contingent is requested
21	Peasant disturbances around Lake Constance
24	Battle of Pavia
27	Formation of the Christian Union in the Allgäu
27-	Drafting of the Twelve Articles commences

March 1	Lake (Constance) band formed
6	Peasant parliament convenes in Memmingen. Formation of the Christian Union – an alliance of the Allgäu, Baltringen and Lake bands.
7	The Federal Ordinance and Twelve Articles are voted through at the Memmingen Peasant Parliament
	The Truchsess reinforces Stuttgart with some 2,200 League troops
8	Ulrich lays siege to Stuttgart
12	Swiss mercenaries abandon Ulrich before Stuttgart
15	Second convening of the Parliament
	Mutiny of the League troops at Dagersheim
17	Duke Ulrich of Württemberg reaches his fortress at Hohentwiel
19	Twelve Articles are printed
22	The Rothenburg militia (Franconia) revolt
25	The Christian Union opens negotiations with the Swabian League in Ulm
26	Peasants storm the monastery in Mergentheim
26	Odenwald peasant band is formed
April 1	First uprising in the Bishopric of Würzburg
2/3	First action by the Allgäu peasants
	In Franconia peasants from Rothenburg, Würzburg and the Tauber valley form an alliance
4	Battle of Leipheim
6	Renewed action by the peasants in Hegau and the Black Forest
12	Bildhausen band, the Nerckar Valley and Odenwald bands are formed
14	Defeat of the peasants at Wurzach
16	Peasant assault on the castle at Weinsberg. Duke Helfenstein is put to death.
17	Treaty of Weingarten
	Formation of the Württemberg band
	Uprising in Gaildorf
	Revolt spreads through Klettgau, Hegau and the Black Forest
21	Duke Ulrich joins the Christian Union
23	Disturbances in the Rhineland Palatinate
24	Georg Truchsess von Waldburg is given orders to march on Würzburg
25	The Württemberg band occupies Stuttgart
27	Götz von Berlichingen joins the main Neckar Valley/ Odenwald band
May 2	Renewed disturbances in the Allgäu
	Uprising in Baden
7	Uprising in Kraichgau
	Tauber Valley band arrives in Heidingsfeld. Start of siege of the Marienberg fortress in Würzburg
8	Peasant articles submitted to the town council of Villingen
12	Defeat of the Württemberg peasants at the Battle of Böblingen
14	Peasant bands converge on Freiburg
21	Weinsberg razed to the ground by the army of the Swabian League

23	Neckar Valley and Odenwald peasant bands give up their siege of Würzburg
24	Freiburg captured by the rebels
26	Götz von Berlichingen abandons peasants
28	Swabian League army repulsed at Neckarsulm
June 2	Battle of Königshofen
4	Peasants cease their siege of Würzburg
	Battle of Ingolstadt
8	Retaking of Würzburg by the League army
9	League occupies Memmingen
11	Reorganisation of the League army
12	Peasants lay siege to Memmingen
17	The Truchsess arrives in Bamberg with the army
18	Cost of campaign estimated at 182,000 florins
27	Allgäu peasants withdraw from Memmingen
July 3	Victory of the Salzburg peasants at Schladming
9	League commences campaign against the Allgäu peasants
14	Defeat of the Allgäu peasants at Leubas
16	Hegau and Black Forest peasants are defeated at Hilzingen
25	The Treaty of Hilzingen
30	The League army occupies Salzburg – Defeat of the Upper Austrian peasants

Preface

I am pleased to have been given the opportunity by Helion to write this book. My interest in the Landsknechts is a long standing one beginning with the basic research I undertook back in 1973 for an Osprey title of the same name. My inspiration to examine this particular group of soldiers and the historical period in which they were active, has in truth, always been driven by a succession of German artists' interpretations of these mercenaries. Emerging during what has been termed the dawn of the early modern era – the period spanning the end of the fifteenth and the beginning of the sixteenth century – the Landsknechts were to remain active until well into the seventeenth century. However, it is arguably during the first quarter of the sixteenth century that these soldiers of fortune gained their notoriety, particularly during the so-called Italian Wars in which they confronted their forerunners – the Swiss *Reisläufer*. The turn of the sixteenth century was accompanied by a flourishing visualisation of social and military life – primarily, but not exclusively, evident in the new medium of the woodcut. Artists were fascinated, if not obsessed, by the new garish costume worn by these fighting men. Some, who served as mercenaries themselves, were able to capture the full horror of war. Others made a living creating bespoke woodcut portraits of individuals – sometimes caricaturing the costume. Some illustrators were commissioned to capture whole inventories of arsenals in colour, others to catalogue the fashion of the day. The upshot is a wealth of visual material which we are only now being able to harvest thanks to the digital capture of these surviving pictorial records. Our ability to understand social and military life during this period has continued to develop as new archive material has been unearthed and, thanks to the brilliance of historians, contextualised into a form which helps us make sense of the realities of military life during this time.

Following the publication of the Osprey title in 1975 I had the good fortune to be working in Germany during the 450th commemoration of the German Peasants' War. This 'revolution of the common man' was one of the most significant events in European history, viewed since as a decisive moment in the development of German parliamentary democracy. Yet it came at a cost of some 100,000 souls crushed during the spring and early summer months of 1525. The commemoration of this conflict had generated a resurgence in Peasants' War research, particularly within the then German

Democratic Republic, but also further afield. Since the Landsknechts fought on both sides, my interest was awoken again and I proceeded to undertake research for a further Osprey title on the armies of the German Peasant War, drawing on the East German research into the military organisation of the peasants.

Some 15 years later I returned to this stomping ground – not having ever given up my interest in the period but now a bit wiser about German society at this time and with a greater repository of visual material on which to draw. The next logical step seemed to me to be an in-depth examination of a particular battle and so I undertook a self-financed book project to research the events surrounding the Battle of Frankenhausen – seen by many historians as perhaps the most decisive engagement of the Peasants' War.

So, when Helion approached me to pen this title for their *From Retinue to Regiment* series it was fortuitous that I had a wealth of background source material. Three titles in particular have been published in German which have really filled in many gaps in our understanding of this period of military history: Reinhard Baumann's 1994 book *Landsknechte*; Mathias Rogg's 2002 title *Landsknechte und Reisläufer: Bilder von Soldaten* and the late Peter Blickle's 2015 biography of Georg von Waldburg: *Der Bauernjörg*. This latter title in particular provides the first detailed account of the campaigns undertaken by the supreme commander of the army of the Swabian League, firstly against the Duke of Württemberg's attempt to retake his duchy, and then to suppress the peasants' uprising in southern Germany, both undertaken in the first half of 1525. This latter work has been indispensable, drawing as it does on the daily accounts of the Truchsess's scribe (later brought to life by Joseph Vochezer), the diary of von Waldburg's herald (Hans Lutz), the Augsburg knight Ambrosius Geyer and the correspondence of the League officials Leonard von Eck and Ulrich Artzt. The level of detail on contingents which has been gleaned from archival records – in particular the League correspondence and the memoirs of Georg von Waldburg – has quite simply been breathtaking and helped me build a picture of the inner workings of a mercenary army at this time. I am also grateful to Dr Reinhard Baumann who has assisted me with some finer points of detail. I have attempted to translate key extracts from the relevant German literature as faithfully as possible but must take responsibility for any factual errors arising from the process.

Doug Miller
Seaton Burn
February 2019

Part I

The Organisation of the League Army

1.1 The Swabian League: Origins

What we know of today as Germany was the largest territory of the Holy Roman Empire during the sixteenth century, the election of office of the Holy Roman Emperor was controlled mostly by German prince-electors who chose one of their peers to become 'King of the Romans' who would later be crowned Emperor by the Pope. The Empire, however, never achieved any great extent of political unification, evolving instead into a decentralised monarchy composed of hundreds of sub-units: kingdoms, principalities, duchies, counties, prince-bishoprics, free Imperial cities, and other domains.

Although most of the elector princes enjoyed a de facto sovereignty within their own territories, they nevertheless owed the Emperor their allegiance since he gave them their authority. The princes thus shared a unifying strategic objective – the maintenance of peace within the defined boundaries of the Empire which in turn secured their legitimacy. Within these boundaries one region had particular strategic importance for the ruling Habsburg dynasty. This was Swabia, a cultural, historic and linguistic region in southwestern Germany. To the east lay Bavaria which was ruled by the expansionist dukes from the House of Wittelsbach. To the south stood the Swiss Confederacy. In order to maintain peace within the territory two political structures had been established – the Swabian League and the Swabian Imperial Circle. The Swabian League, which predates the establishment of the Imperial Circle, was formed in 1487 following a mandate from the Emperor Friedrich III of Habsburg. Somewhat later in 1500 during the reign of Maximilian I, the Swabian Circle was established as one of six Imperial circles at the Diet of Augsburg to safeguard the 'Perpetual Public Peace' proclaimed in 1495, enforcing the verdicts of the Imperial Chamber Court, collecting Imperial taxes, and raising troops for the Empire.

At the first constituent assembly of the Swabian League – the Imperial Diet at Esslingen – 22 Imperial cities, the Swabian knights' League of St George's Shield, bishops, and princes (Ansbach, Baden, Bavaria, Bayreuth, Hesse, Mainz, the Electorate of the Palatinate, Trier, Tyrol, and Württemberg)

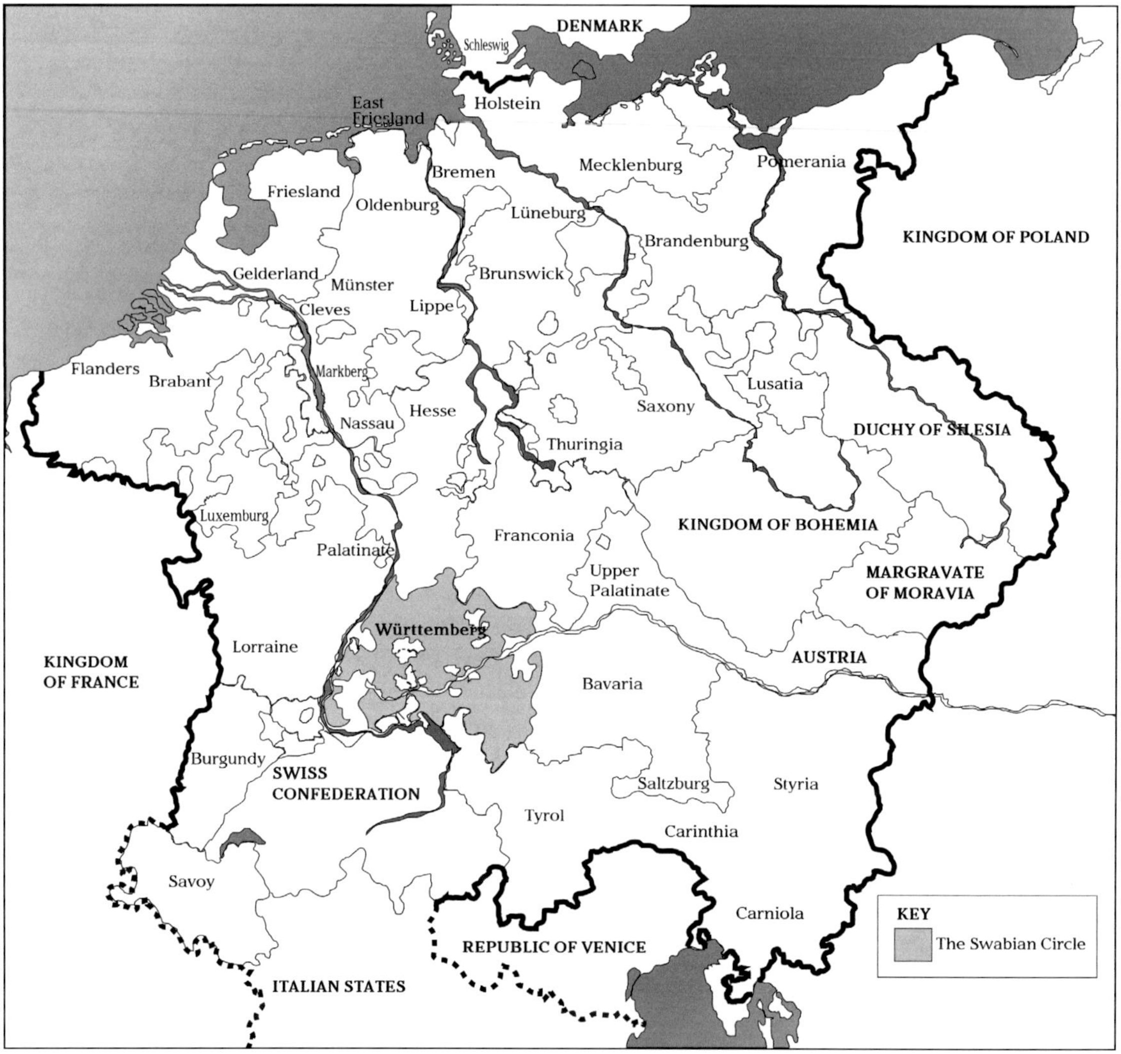

Map 1. The Swabian circle. This map shows the various Imperial circles within the Holy Roman Empire and the political faultlines running within the Swabian circle. Substantial pockets of the territory belonged to the Habsburgs and were governed by Archduke Ferdinand in Austria. As peasant disturbances spread from these domains to other parts of the region – notably Upper Swabia – Ferdinand felt compelled to bring the matter to the attention of the Swabian League.

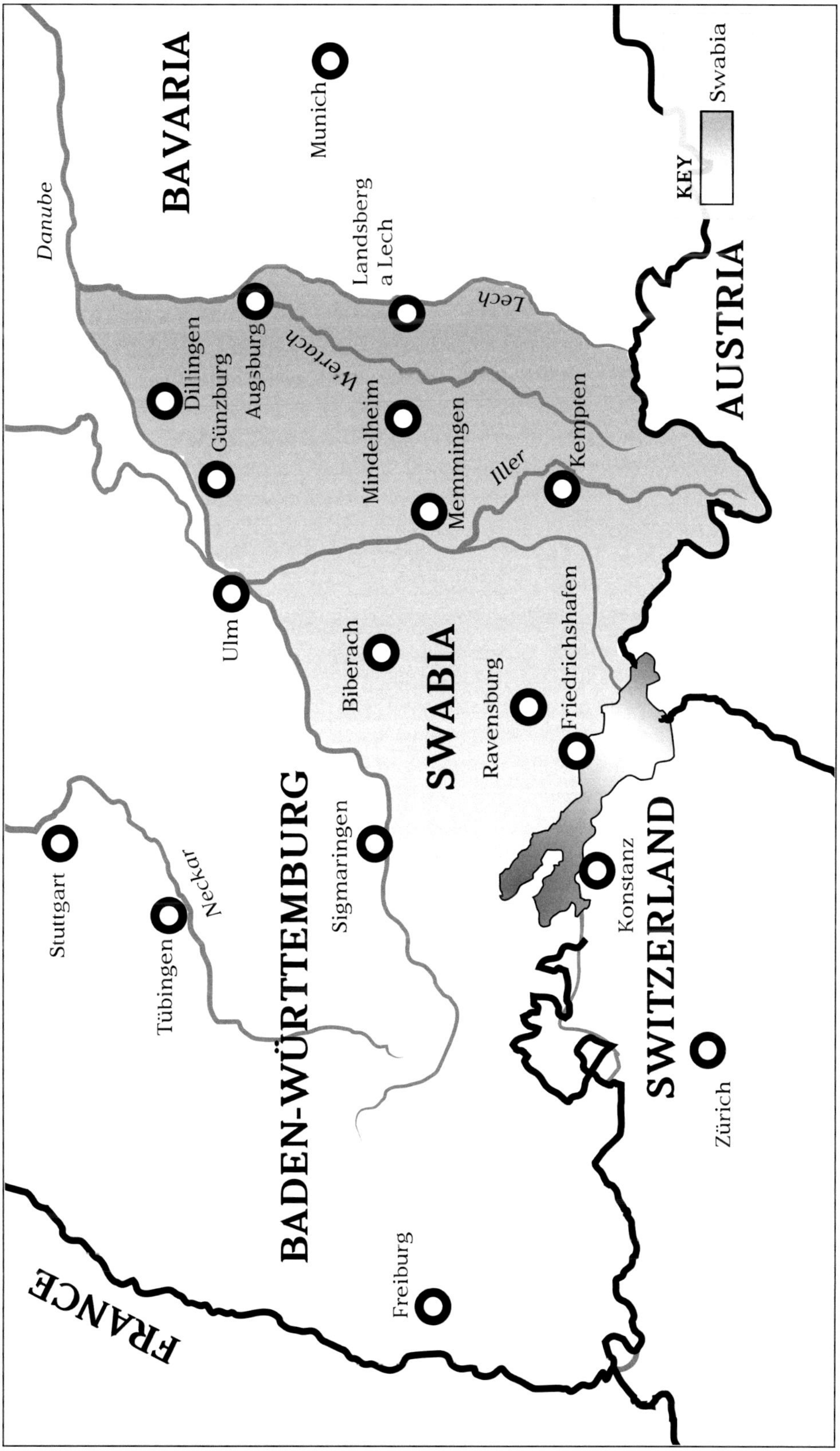

Map 2. Swabia in 1525. Bordered by France, Switzerland and Bavaria, Swabia was of great strategic importance to the south of the Holy Roman Empire.

came together in a defensive association charged with maintaining peace within the territory. From the outset it had been clear that such an alliance would require periodic renewal, and on subsequent occasions new members came into the fold: notably the bishoprics of Mainz, Würzburg, Bamberg, and Salzburg as well as the secular principalities of Austria, Bavaria, and Bayreuth and a number of Imperial cities, notably Nuremberg, Strasbourg, and Rothenburg.

As the League developed it proved necessary to create an appropriate administrative apparatus and organisational structure consisting of a League executive (*Bundeshauptleute*), a League judiciary (*Bundesrichter*), a council, (*Bundesrat*) and a members' assembly (*Bundesversammlung*). The League Council consisted of a three-man executive: Wilhelm Güss von Güssenberg representing the nobility, Walter von Hirnheim covering the ecclesiastical dignitaries and Ulrich Artzt, spokesman for the cities and 21 members, seven each from the three estates. It met regularly at Ulm and occasionally at Augsburg. The League chancellor was the Bavarian hardliner Leonard von Eck. The League had its own war council which numbered seven, including the chancellor with two members from each estate. The membership of the council of war could rotate but the chancellor remained a permanent member. These organs were key decision-making bodies but were also used to settle disputes between members. By 1523,when a unification renewal was set for a further 11 years, the League's reach extended across most of southern Germany and it functioned as an important political bloc within the Empire.

Following the peace of 1499 with the Swiss and the resounding defeat of the aggressive Wittelsbachs in 1504, the League's original purpose – maintenance of the status quo in the south-west – could be accomplished. However, new tensions were soon to arise, tensions which emanated from the actions of Ulrich, Duke of Württemberg. Ulrich V had succeeded his kinsman Eberhard II as Duke of Württemberg in 1498, and was awarded territories from the Palatinate as reward for his military service on behalf of the Holy Roman Emperor Maximilian I and the Wittelsbachs of Bavaria. In 1511 Ulrich had married Sabina, a daughter of Albert IV, Duke of Bavaria, of the Wittelsbach dynasty. Sabina was the niece of the Emperor Maximilian and sister of the future Duke Wilhelm IV of Bavaria. However, Ulrich's courtly largesse plunged him deeply into debt and he became very unpopular with his subjects, provoking the peasant insurrection known as the 'Poor Conrad' uprising in 1514 triggered by the introduction of new taxes and dubious weights and measures. In the ensuing Treaty of Tübingen he assumed liability for his debts and granted the Estates important rights, but barely addressed the outstanding peasant grievances. Ulrich's marriage to Sabina was a very unhappy one, and having formed an affection for the wife of a knight named Hans von Hutten, the Duke murdered him during an altercation. Hutten's friends now rallied in opposition to the Duke and Sabina sought refuge from her husband with the Emperor and her brother Wilhelm. Duke Ulrich was twice subjected to an Imperial ban. When Maximilian died in January 1519, Ulrich found himself isolated within the region. He had already renounced his membership of the League and following the murder of Hans von Hutten in 1515, had become the object of much scorn from his contemporaries. When he laid siege to the city of Reutlingen with plans to take others in his duchy in the same year, the League was duly compelled to mobilise and tasked Georg Truchsess[1] of Waldburg with his expulsion from Württemberg.

After a failed attempt to retake Stuttgart in May 1519, Ulrich renewed his efforts in August but he had underestimated the military power of the League which still controlled the majority of cities and castles in his territory. By October Ulrich's supplies had been exhausted and he was forced to leave his duchy. Once in exile, to cover the costs of their campaign, the League sold his duchy to the new Emperor Charles V, who in turn granted the territory to his brother, Archduke Ferdinand. The Archduke, however, had been slow to transfer funds to the League which became a source of ongoing tension within its membership.

1.1 The Swabian League coat of arms 1522 with the motto 'What God has joined let man not separate', and featuring the Cross of St George which featured on the League standard. Coloured Woodcut by Hans Burgkmair the Elder (1473–1531). (Courtesy: Staatsbibliothek München)

While Ulrich was languishing in Switzerland plotting his return, a new challenge to peace within the League manifested itself in the unruly actions of the robber barons of Franconia. In the summer of 1523, responding to a request from the city of Nuremberg, the League felt compelled to take action against 23 knights in Franconia who had supported Thomas von Absberg – notorious for his kidnapping and ransoming of merchants and Imperial diplomats as they travelled between Nuremberg and Augsburg.[2]

By the summer of 1524 a new and potentially more threatening danger confronted the League. The activities of rogue princes and knights could be contained but across much Southern Germany the municipalities and the peasant masses were stirring. Changes had been occurring in the economy of the Holy Roman Empire in the new modern era. The cities and towns – as new centres of processing and distribution – were generating different social classes – wealthy patricians and burghers (merchants), artisans and urban day workers. Where municipalities remained under the control of the nobility, rights issues and taxation became a major bone of contention and political tensions began to surface.

1 Senechal or steward.

2 The military actions of the League army were captured in 23 woodcuts by the artist Hans Wandereisen <https://de.wikipedia.org/wiki/Wandereisen-Holzschnitte_von_1523> (accessed 6 November 2018).

1.2 Duke Ulrich of Württemberg (1487–1550), a profligate and unpopular ruler of the Duchy which he lost in 1519 having been exiled by the Swabian League with the sanction of the Holy Roman Emperor. His support for the Reformation and his efforts to retake his territory by forming an alliance with the Swiss and disaffected peasantry prompted the mobilisation of the League army in 1525.

Beyond the walls of the cities and towns at the foot of the social order were the peasants, who although they had their own social hierarchy, carried the burden of all the other strata of society:

> Whether the peasant was the subject of a prince, an Imperial baron, a bishop, a monastery or a city, he was everywhere treated as a beast of burden, and worse. If he was a serf, he was entirely at the mercy of his master. If he was a bondsman, the legal deliveries stipulated by agreement were sufficient to crush him; even they were being daily increased. Most of his time, he had to work on his master's estate. Out of that which he earned in his few free hours, he had to pay tithes, dues, ground rents, war taxes, land taxes, Imperial taxes, and other payments. He could neither marry nor die without paying the master.[3]

A heady mix of increased taxes, failed harvests, a steadily growing list of unaddressed grievances and the impact of radical reformist theology had fuelled a number of peasant disturbances in the years leading up to 1525 and matters were now coming to a boiling point.

When the peasant disturbances began to spread in late Autumn 1524, the affected areas were primarily in those Habsburg territories between the Black Forest and Lake Constance formerly belonging to the Duke of Württemberg. The military response was initiated by Archduke Ferdinand of Austria. At the League Assembly in Ulm on 28 October 1524 his commissioners were compelled to report to the League on the gravity of the peasant disturbances in the district of Waldshut which the Archduke had hoped to suppress himself:

> But since the affair has turned out vexatiously in so many ways, his Highness was moved to bring it before the Estates [of the Swabian League]. So we request in his Highness's name … that you will take the matter to heart and be moved [by the thought that] if this disobedience goes unpunished, all the subjects and allies [of the Estates of the Swabian League] will receive a bad example of disobedience, especially those inclined to evil, and will undertake similar deeds against their rulers; for if it is not stopped at the outset the wickedness will increase, and in the end resistance [to it] will be the more painful.[4]

However, apart from a minor confrontation at Donauwörth on 13 December, there was little military response on the part of the League.

3 Friedrich Engels, *The Peasant War in Germany* (London: Lawrence and Wishart, 1850), p. 39.

4 Karl Klüpfel, 'Urkunden zur Geschichte des Schwäbischen Bundes (1488–1533)', in T. Scott and R.Scribner (eds), *The German Peasants' War. A History in Documents* (Amherst: Prometheus Books, 1991), p. 150.

Military Organisation of the League

1.3 Archduke Ferdinand (1503–1564). Before his accession, he ruled the Austrian hereditary lands of the Habsburgs in the name of his elder brother, Charles V, Holy Roman Emperor and served as his representative in Germany. Portrait by Jan Cornelisz Vermeyen. (Courtesy: Fondation Bemberg. Photo: Didier Descouens)

Defending the interests of the nobility, clergy and the Imperial city, members of the League would require considerable resources and the League Council knew that they would not be able to fall back on the support of the Holy Roman Emperor (now Charles V) since he was wholly committed to waging his war against Francis I in Italy. The defence of home territory and the interests of the estates would therefore have to be self-financed. It had been realised at an early stage that it would be necessary to draw up very precise rules for military engagement particularly in relation to expected member contingents. Having fixed the overall size of what was deemed to be an appropriate military force at 1,845 horse and 10,835 foot,[5] the League Council would then determine how large the mobilisation should be to address any perceived military threat. Contingents might be declared in thirds, quarters or fifths of the total troops required and each member was then charged with providing a percentage of the total share and to ensuring that these men appeared at the appointed muster. It was agreed that in certain circumstances, the Council might waive such an obligation in return for an appropriate sum of money. When the first peasant disturbances occurred late in October 1524, the Council laid down the precise numbers which were to make up a one-quarter contingent: 463 mounted men-at-arms and 2,746 infantry.

Table 1. One Quarter League Contingent

Member	Horse	Foot
Austria (Habsburg)	50	400
Archbishopric of Mainz	25	100
Palatinate	75	200
Bishopric of Bamberg	25	63
Bishopric of Würzburg	38	125
Bishopric of Eichstätt	10	56
Bishopric of Augsburg	10	62
Bishopric of Constance	3	15
Duke of Bavaria	50	350
Margrave of Ansbach-Kulmbach	25	100
Landgrave of Hesse	63	100
Duchy of Württemberg	25	200
Knights of St George	13	250
Nuremberg incl. Windshein	18	150
Other cities	33	575

Source: Siegfried Hoyer: 109

5 Peter Blickle, *Der Bauernjörg* (C.H. Beck: Munich, 2015), p. 313.

Since there had been tensions in the past over the failure of certain members to honour their required contingents, special measures had to be undertaken; as in 1519, when dedicated officers (*Musterherren*) were appointed to oversee each muster, to avoid any double counting or ghosting,[6] and ensure that the correct number of troops had been sent.

The situation changed however in the early months of 1525 as mass uprisings occurred across south-west Germany. On 5 February the League executive called for a mobilisation of its members with a request that they recruit one-third of their full contingents. However, it took six days before this could be agreed, by which time the second third was required to be on standby. Units were ordered to assemble in the environs of the city of Ulm. On 12 February Ulrich Artzt, secretary of the League, reported to the authorities in Ulm that he expected the army to have assembled by the 27th of that month. The League Council expected 1,045 horse and 2,407 foot but Artzt expressed concern that the size of the initial muster would be no match for the steadily expanding horde of peasant rebels in the region. The initial response of the League members resulted in a preponderance of mounted men-at-arms, with Philipp of Hesse[7] and the Bavarian nobility offering horse only. Konrad von Thüngen, Prince-Bishop of Würzburg, had sent 105 knights and four wagons.[8] Whereas the League members from the nobility could more readily offer horse from their retinues, the city members were more likely to offer infantry, finding it difficult to recruit mounted men. Augsburg, for example, had to recruit in the surrounding area just to meet its quota of 18. The secretary expressed his disappointment that Ulm was unable to provide half the required number of horse. The quality of infantry proved to be varied. Whereas Augsburg was able to recruit seasoned Landsknechts for the first roll call, those foot soldiers present in the Bavarian contingent proved to have had little combat experience, and the captain reported to Leonard von Eck that a number had deserted. Eck demanded that they be made an example of.

1.4 Leonard von Eck (1480–1550) was Chancellor to William IV of Bavaria and a powerful opponent of the Reformation. He played a leading role in the chancellery of the Swabian League. (Courtesy: Metropolitan Museum of Art)

By now however, there was a new additional threat to the League. Duke Ulrich had returned from his exile in Switzerland and France intent on recovering his duchy. Having announced his conversion to the Protestant faith a year previously, he felt this would enable him to build support from a disgruntled peasantry roused by radical reformist clerics. Having assembled an army of Swiss and French mercenaries

6 Reinhard Baumann, *Landsknechte* (Munich: C.H. Beck Verlag, 1994), p. 76.

7 Wilhelm Falckenheiner, *Philipp Der Grossmütige Im Bauernkriege* (Kessinger Publishing, 1887/2010), p. 3.

8 Ambrosius Geyer quoted in Franz Ludwig Baumann (ed.), *Quellen zur Geschichte des Bauernkrieges in Oberschwaben* (Tübingen: Literarischer Verein, 1877), p. 723.

he invaded Württemberg in February 1525, and ensconced his army at the fortress of Hohentwiel.

This posed considerable problems for the League, which had to find the necessary finance to meet a second roll call to conduct this impending war against Ulrich and to deal with the peasant uprising at the same time. As the dispute with Duke Ulrich reached its climax, the League demanded the third roll call in money rather than men in order to pay those existing troops in the field and to recruit additional units. In the meantime, Archduke Ferdinand was at pains to keep his commander duly financed to prosecute the peasants in his territories:

> Our government in Ensisheim has informed us that five thousand florins will be paid over on 3 March against your receipt. At your request, two culverins are being sent to you immediately, and our councillor Christoph Fuchs has detailed further horse and foot to strengthen the garrison at Stockach.
>
> Enclosure: We inform you that we have arranged to borrow ten thousand florins from the Fuggers.[9]

Although the subsequent collapse of Ulrich's campaign in March 1525 eased the financial pressure on the League, on 28 March the council was nevertheless compelled to notify its members that in meeting the first two roll calls there had been serious shortcomings in the contingents mobilised by the municipalities. Moreover, the army would have to step up its efforts in the field to self-finance by means of extortion – so-called *Brandschatzung* – by which the peasant communities would be threatened with the razing of their property unless they handed over money.

1.2 The Command Structure within the League Army

By the turn of the sixteenth century the nobility, which had been responsible for defence in medieval times, was slowly losing its military standing as the development of new techniques of infantry combat began to diminish the effectiveness of the mounted knight on the battlefield. Yet the values of knighthood remained the glue which kept the established order in place. No person was more aware of this than the Holy Roman Emperor Maximilian I (1459–1519) who fervently upheld the principles of chivalry and was keen to see that the nobility held on to these traditions. He commissioned three biographical books during his lifetime – the *Weisskunig* (White King), the *Theuerdank* (noble or knightly thought), and a book of tournaments entitled *Freydal*. All three were printed as woodcuts and distributed to his members of court. In these works, the virtues of closeness with nature pursued via the hunt, physical prowess as expressed in the tournament, and loyalty to church and state were extolled as the ideals of chivalric society. Alongside

9 Letter from Archduke Ferdinand to the Truchsess dated March 3, in Scott and Scribner, p. 153.

these assets a knight was expected to have diplomatic and legal know-how as well as a knowledge of the workings of the institutions of the Empire.

Territorial organisations of the knighthood predated the formation of the Swabian League. The Brotherhood of the Knights of St George, which had been formed by a group of upper Swabian knights in 1406, had endured following the establishment and renewal of the Swabian League and remained as a separate tightly knit grouping within the League, much to the displeasure of Charles V and senior League officials.[10]

Despite this political manoeuvre, knight commanders were subordinate to the League politicians who were their contractors. The League had made provision for a seven-man council of war (*Kriegsrat*) comprising two representatives from each estate and presided over by the Bavarian chancellor Leonard von Eck. Strategic decisions were made in Ulm but as the campaign progressed it became a peripatetic body which met up with the commander in the field. Generally, it would consist of a rotating three-man delegation, who were there to advise the supreme commander on matters of strategy. As far as decision-making in the field was concerned, as we shall see, despite the rise of infantry tactics, the mounted warrior still had a major role to play in the eyes of the knight commander, particularly against their own subjects who were not expected to be well drilled in the use of pike.

Following the peasant uprisings in the Klettgau and Hegau areas in June 1524, the order was given by Archduke Ferdinand to suppress all such disturbances in his territories in Württemberg and Lower Austria. Georg Truchsess von Waldburg was appointed supreme commander. Following an education in Augsburg and Freiburg, von Waldburg had received a diplomatic training alongside his uncle Eitelfried von Zollern who introduced him at an early stage in his career to Charles V and Archduke Ferdinand. His first military experience came at the age of 21 in the Augsburg Wars of Succession of 1508. Later he supported the Duke of Württemberg in 1514 in suppressing the Poor Conrad peasant uprising in the Rems Valley near Stuttgart. Under the terms of his commission he was expected to muster 100 horse and 600 foot. Two years later we find him in Italy as supreme commander of the Bavarian contingent serving Maximilian in the Venetian Wars. In 1519 Austria succeeded in recruiting the Truchsess away from his Bavarian commission, and in 1520 offered his services to the Swabian League of which it was a member. There he received a new contract as supreme commander with a monthly stipend of 400 florins. In his first major action for the League we find him in Franconia during the Absberg feud of 1523.

By this time the League had become a very well-oiled administrative machine. In 1512 it had created a set of new positions within the army – a paymaster (*Pfennigmeister*), recruitment officers to oversee the muster (*Musterherren*) and a provost marshal (*Profoss*) responsible for maintaining order and meting out punishment. These new ranks were adopted for the whole of the Empire in 1522 and eventually mirrored by the peasants in their

10 Gabriele von Trauchburg, 'Gefechte und Schlachten – die Kontrahenten und die Ereignisse', in Elmar Kuhn (ed.), *Der Bauernkrieg in Oberschwaben* (Tübingen: Bibliotheca Academia-Verlag, 2000) pp. 175–198.

own military organisation (see Appendix I). Some positions had already been filled by the League but senior officers now had to be appointed by the Truchsess Georg von Waldburg. Wilhelm von Fürstenberg was given overall command of the infantry while Frowen von Hutten took command of the horse. Michael Ott von Echterdingen was appointed to supreme commander of the ordnance while Jos von Laubenberg took command of the vanguard light horse or *Rennfahne* as it was known. In addition, appointments were made to the ranks of quartermaster (*Quartiermeister*) notably Wilhelm von Baldeck and Heinrich Treusch von Beutler, and fire master (*Brandmeister*)[11] in the person of Burkhardt Heinrich. The latter was an important rank developed to extort monies from the citizenry on pain of seeing their dwellings razed to the ground.

1.5. Georg 'Truchsess' von Waldburg (1488–1531). The term *Truchsess* translates as steward. A military contractor and supreme commander who between 1508 and 1515 served Duke Ulrich von Württemberg, helping him to supress the Poor Conrad rebellion of 1514. In 1516 he fought for Bavaria alongside Maximilian I, Holy Roman Emperor, in Italy against France and their allies. In 1525 as supreme commander of the Swabian League he pursued Duke Ulrich following the latter's attempt to retake his duchy, and subsequently led the campaign against the peasants of Upper Swabia and Franconia. The following year he received the hereditary title Reichserbtruchsess (Imperial Steward) from the Emperor Charles V. (Photo: Andreas Präfcke)

One of the most challenging command tasks fell to Wilhelm von Fürstenberg, who had to deal with an odd mix of rank-and-file mercenaries. In 1521, at the age of 30, he had entered the service of Francis I of France, where for an annual salary of 6,000 livres he was awarded supreme command of the German and Swiss mercenaries in French service and tasked with protecting the Burgundian territories. This marked his entry into the world of mercenary warfare. Because the house of Fürstenberg had maintained a longstanding feud with Duke Ulrich of Württemberg, when news broke that the latter was seeking to retake control of the Duchy, Fürstenberg offered 2,000 men to the League to suppress the Duke's manoeuvres. The League required little persuasion in appointing him commander of their infantry. He remained with the League during the campaign against Ulrich and the peasants even though his territories were suffering economically as a result of the conflicts. It is estimated that the House of Fürstenberg lost some 30,000 florins during this time. Despite this, or arguably because of this, he was inclined to be more lenient towards his subjects lest further misery prevent his tenants from recovering to a position where he would be able to profit from their labours.[12] When the League army was disbanded, Wilhelm von Fürstenberg was tasked with announcing this to his men in the absence of the Truchsess. The

11 There is no real equivalent for this rank, which involved the extortion of monies from those deemed to have participated in rebellious activity on threat of their dwellings being razed to the ground.

12 Johannes Volker Wagner *Graf Wilhelm von Furstenberg 1491–1549 und die politisch-geistigen Mächte und Ereignisse seiner Zeit*, (Stuttgart: Anton Hiersemann, 1966) pp 20–32.

1.6. Wilhelm von Fürstenberg (1491–1549), commander of the League infantry. Lithographie by Claude Régnier based on an oil painting in Heiligenberg Castle (probable date 1850). (Courtesy: The Fuerstenberg House Archive)

League thanked him for his efforts, particularly in dealing with the threatened mutinies at Leipheim and Königshofen.

Von Fürstenberg was dependent on his men abiding by the strict military code laid down in the articles of war or so-called field ordinances (see Appendix I). These established ranks and rules which men were expected to observe under oath. Provided the men were paid, order could prevail but rules of engagement were often difficult to uphold, particularly where a victorious army, intent on plunder to enhance its earnings, could go on a rampage. As we shall see later, the League was at pains to keep its infantry in particular in check. In a mercenary army much of this depended of course on a well-endowed war chest.

1.3 The League Horse

The League horse was placed under the command of Froben (aka Frowen) von Hutten (1469–1529), cousin of Ulrich von Hutten. Frowen was less experienced in military matters than his counterparts in the command group but had a score to settle with Duke Ulrich of Württemberg, who had murdered his brother Hans von Hutten a decade earlier. As commander of the horse he was second in command of the League army, which indicated the importance attached to armoured mounted men-at-arms and lighter 'free lancers' who were to prove crucial in the ensuing campaign against the peasants. Beneath his rank there were rotating commanders of the so-called *Rennfahne*[13] – the unit of horse chosen to take up position either at the head of a column or in the front rank of a battle. The term *Rennfahne* refers to the custom at the investiture of a prince, whereby the candidate would gallop around the seated Holy Roman Emperor three times (the so-called *Berennung*) whereupon on the second and third passings, the Imperial standard and the heraldic standard of the family in question respectively would be placed before the Emperor.[14] The initial commander of the League *Rennfahne* was Jos von Laubenberg.[15] Since this was not an Imperial army as such, we can surmise that the League *Rennfahne* would either have borne the heraldry

13 The *Reichsrennfahne* was the Imperial battle flag of the Holy Roman Emperor carried by the front rank, characterised by two crossed red swords on a black and silver background.

14 <http://www.welt-der-wappen.de/Heraldik/rennfahne.htm> (accessed 1 October 2018).

15 Later substituted in turn by Burckhardt Heinrich, Marschal von Pappenheim and Wolf Dietrich von Homburg.

of von Laubenberg or perhaps that of the Swabian League, rather than the insignia of crossed red swords on a black and white background.

Generally, the League horse was recruited from within the nobility. As far as warfare was concerned at this time, the 'well born', well-equipped, aristocratic horseman was still broadly assumed to be the single most powerful combatant on the battlefield. Each noble was accompanied by a number of mounted men-at-arms whom he could freely call upon. These were the so-called *Lehnsleute*, i.e. those vassals obliged to demonstrate their loyalty to their liege lord by rendering their services in combat for which they would be rewarded either by a grant of land (a fief or *Lehen*), or by receiving an office. The life of a *Lehnsmann* in the early sixteenth century was described quite vividly by Ulrich von Hutten (1488–1523) in a letter to Nuremberg lawyer Willibald Pirckheimer (1470–1530). In 1499 Pirckheimer had been chosen by the City Council to command their contingent of troops in the Imperial army during the Swabian War against the Swiss:

> We [also] serve a prince, from whom we hope for protection; … In addition, for the prince's liegeman, this hope [of protection] is combined every day with danger and fear. For if I put just one foot out of the house, there is the risk that I will come across people with whom the prince has had disputes and feuds, and that they will attack me and take me away as a prisoner. If I am unlucky, I could lose half my possessions to pay the ransom and so the protection I am supposed to enjoy would turn out to be quite the opposite.
>
> We therefore keep horses and buy ourselves weapons, and surround ourselves with a large retinue, all of which costs a great deal of money. We cannot leave even two acres of land unguarded for very long, we must not visit a farm without being armed, and, when hunting and fishing, we have to wear armour.[16]

1.7. This woodcut by Erhard Schön depicts light horsemen in procession. As with foot soldiers many of these were 'free lancers' who sold their services to military contractors. Note the substantial baggage carried by the horseman in the foreground and the burgonet helmets.

Appendix IV shows the composition of the Austrian contingent of horse provided by Archduke Ferdinand with their liegemen (horse) on the eve of the Battle of Leipheim 2 April 1525. At the head of this unit of horse were the principal commanders of the army. Records show that this contingent alone cost 27,589 florins to keep in the field for the duration of the campaign.[17]

16 Ulrich von Hutten, (1518). Extract from a letter to Willibald Pirckheimer, dated 25 October 1518, Marburg Digital Archive <http://www.digam.net/document.php?dok=1275> (accessed 1 August 2018).

17 Blickle, p. 301.

Even though this was a territorial League contingent, the disparate nature of the units of men who came together in this company would have necessitated considerable coordination and discipline. Where a contingent of horse was formed of units from different territories, the command would rotate. The Bishops of Mainz, Bamberg and Würzburg each provided 100 men with their own captains who exchanged command of the entire 300-strong unit on a daily basis. The mounted men-at-arms supplied by the Elector of Palatine (300), his brother Friedrich (40) and the Dukes Ottheinrich and Philipp (27) were commanded by the knights von Fleckenstein and von Schemberg. Duke William of Bavaria and the Margrave Casimir of Brandenburg together recruited 300 men under the joint command of Ulrich Marschal von Pappenheim and von Wolfstein while Philipp of Hesse supplied 200 men under the command of Sigmund von Bemmelberg. The Bishops of Eichstätt and Augsburg as well the priories, nobles and Imperial Cities were under the rotating command of Lienhard von Gundelsheim and Diepold von Stein.[18]

Table 2. Contingents and Financial Contributions

Member	Horse	Foot	Monthly amount in Florins
Austria	200	1,600	8,800
Mainz	100	400	2,800
Palatinate	300	800	6,800
Bamberg	100	252	2,200
Würzburg	152	500	2,800
Eichstätt	40	224	1,380
Augsburg	40	248	1,480
Constance	12	60	384
Bavaria	200	1,400	8,000
Brandenburg	100	400	2,800
Hesse	252	400	4,600
Württemberg	100	800	4,400
Knights	52	1000	4,600
Nuremberg incl. Windshein	72	600	3,240
Other cities	132	2,300	8,800
Total	1,852	10,984	67,844

These figures conflict with those estimates of Ulrich Artzt,[19] who put the number of the League horse at 1,500 whereas Ambrosius Geyer placed the figure at 1,800.[20] In addition to the *Rennfahne* and these units of League horse there was a contingent of Austrian horse consisting of 500 men-at-arms directly under the command of the Truchsess, who appointed Duke Ulrich

18 Blickle, p. 149.

19 Ulrich Artzt quoted in Wilhelm Vogt, *Die Correspondenz des schwäbischen Bundeshauptmanns Ulrich Artzt von Augsburg aus den Jahren 1524 und 1525: ein Beitrag zur Geschichte des Bauernkrieges in Schwaben* (Augsburg: Himmer 1880), p. 387.

20 Ambrosius Geyer Handlung, *Des Bundes wider die Bauern in Baumann F.L,.* p. 725.

of Helfenstein as their captain and ensign (see Appendix IV).[21] It would seem that the League had as much difficulty in raising contingents of horse as they did infantry. Sections of the nobility were clearly concerned about parting with men whom they required to defend their own territory. Gerwig Blarer, president of the bench of prelates in the Swabian League who was charged with helping to recruit troops for the League's army wrote to his brother the Abbot of Weingarten:

> Dear brother Gerwig since you write that I should engage some horse, let me tell you that in God's truth I do not know how to find any. Truchsess Georg has a great troop of horse with him. The devil take all horsemen! There are none available. By God, I know of no more than two mounted soldiers I could send for, have neither horses nor men. Things hereabouts are such that we need men here with us rather than send them away. Therefore, dear brother, we are pondering how to get hold of horsemen. If some nobleman is commanded to raise a hundred horse on our behalf, which I think necessary I shall inform you without delay ...[22]

Generally the Imperial city members were more likely to provide infantry. However, they had divided loyalties when it came to mobilising against the peasants. Leonard von Eck had already anticipated this eventuality and had suggested to Duke Wilhelm of Bavaria that he should recruit further afield – notably in Bohemia. The chancellor even suggested the deployment of *Stradiots* – mounted troops of Albanian and Greek origin who had initially entered Venetian military service during the Republic's wars with the Ottoman Empire in the fifteenth century.[23] This was undertaken with limited success as far as the League was concerned although somewhat belatedly, and at greater expense than normal. Duke Wilhelm reinforced his border with the Allgäu until the end of July with 1,000 of these men.[24]

This notwithstanding, by the end of March between 1,500 and 1,800 mounted men had mustered, constituting about two-thirds of the roll decreed by the League on 28 October 1524. There is little direct information about the state of equipment and armour borne by the League horse. We must assume that those knights present in the ranks would have been clad in full body armour – those who could still afford it would either have had

21 These men were later replaced by Duke Friedrich of Fürstenberg and Wolf von Homburg respectively.

22 Christoph Blarer to his Brother, Gerwig Blarer, Abbot of Weingarten, 18 February 1525. Gerwig Blarer, president of the bench of prelates in the Swabian League, was charged with helping to recruit troops for the League's army, but anxious at the same time to protect his own territory against the rebellion. Blarer, Briefe und Akten I, 35–36 (no. 59), quoted in Scott and Scribner p. 151

23 Nicholas C.J. Pappas, '*Stradioti*: Balkan Mercenaries In Fifteenth And Sixteenth Century Italy', 2015 <https://www.scribd.com/document/150901226/STRADIOTI-BALKAN-MERCENARIES-IN-FIFTEENTH-AND-SIXTEENTH-CENTURY-ITALY-By-Nicholas-C-J-Pappas> (accessed 25 July 2018).

24 Johann Edmund Jörg, *Deutschland in der Revolutionsperiode von 1522 bis 1526* (Freiburg in Breisgau:Herder'sche Verlagsbuchhandlung, 1851), quoted in Siegfried Hoyer, *Das Militärwesen im deutschen Bauernkrieg 1524–1526* (Berlin: Deutscher Militärverlag, 1975), p. 131.

1.8. The stradioti, mounted troops of Albanian and Greek origin, initially entered Venetian military service during the Republic's wars with the Ottoman Empire in the fifteenth century, but were also employed in southern Germany. They appear in numerous contemporary woodcuts and pioneered light cavalry tactics in the early modern era, employing hit-and-run tactics, ambushes, feigned retreats and other complex manoeuvres. (Woodcut: Jörg Breu)

1.9. Referred to somewhat misleadingly as 'Maximilian' style because its development coincided with the Emperor's reign, this armour extended the decorative ridges and grooves which had appeared in the earlier 'Gothic' form into major feature which ran vertically up all the main elements of the suit. Known as 'fluting' it offered extra protection against blows. (Courtesy: Metropolitan Museum of Art)

full suits of Maximilian armour made in the workshops of Augsburg or the smoother armour made in Milan. Contemporary images show mounted men-at-arms partially clad in armour often under a frock coat (see Plate 4).

We have a description from Georg von Waldburg's scribe of the march formation of the League army as it broke camp at Erbach near Ulm:

> At the head of the vanguard was the Rennfahne [under Jos von Laubenberg]. This was followed by a company of handgunners and a section of the artillery. The main part of the van comprised the forlorn hope '*verlorene Haufe*' and 3 squadrons of horse which changed their positions every three days. There then followed the main artillery train behind which marched the main column of infantry or *Gewalthaufen*. To the rear followed 2 more companies of horse and the munitions wagons and the baggage train (*Tross*). The latter were covered by a further company of horse.[25]

1.10. This woodcut shows the different types of mounted men at arms in an army at this time. The front rank would be heavily armoured, clad from head to toe in a full set of armour with a barded horse followed by lighter cavalry in armour but with no steel protection for the horses. To the rear is the light horse with virtually no armour whatsoever. (Woodcut: Erhard Schön)

Hoyer has calculated that a company of, for example,120 mounted horsemen organised in three squadrons allowing for five metres for each horse including a gap would have required some 200 metres.[26] This latter unit would have struggled to carry out its orders given the nature of the baggage train which would stretch out into the distance in an unordered fashion. The army must have been an immense sight.

Tactical deployment of horse was in a state of flux at this time as mounted men-at-arms could be successfully repulsed by a well-drilled pike square or *gevierte Ordnung* and picked off by hand-gunners in the wings. Despite this emerging superiority of the infantry at this time, the military success of the League as we shall see was to owe much to the engagement of its light horsemen and mobile artillery. In some cases, the light horse was backed up with what appear to be mobile arquebusiers. Although it is not clear from contemporary accounts of the League army, we know that the Duke of Lorraine ordered his arquebusiers to ride with his heavy horse and dismount to engage with the peasants of Alsace at the battle of Sauverne.[27] We must surmise that

25 Joseph Vogeser, *Geschichte des fürstlichen Hauses Waldburg in Schwaben Vol 2* (Kempten:188), p. 547, quoted in Hoyer p. 116.

26 Hoyer, op.cit., p. 131.

27 Manfred Bensing and Siegfried Hoyer, *Der Deutsche Bauernkrieg* (Berlin: Deutscher Militärverlag:1982), p. 116.

1.11. Officer of the Muster – appointed by the League to police the recruitment process, which could result in all manner of sharp practices. Note the rather hefty purse carried over the saddle. (Woodcut: Erhard Schön)

this tactic was also used by the Truchsess, where battle conditions required a rapid deployment of arquebusiers. Few woodcuts show mounted men-at-arms carrying handguns or arquebuses at this time. In any event reloading on horseback would have been virtually impossible, most certainly in close quarter combat. Despite the presence of Landsknechts in the ranks of the peasants, and peasant roll calls itemising polearms, the pike does not seem to have been adopted wholesale as the rebel weapon of choice against the League light horse. Accounts relate how the rebels preferred to take up defensive positions behind their circled wagons and carts. As we shall see later, such peasant defences tended to be easily outflanked by the deployment of light horse in most of the engagements with the League army.

This tactic of rapidly deploying the *Rennfahne* was preferred by Georg von Waldburg for several reasons. Firstly, it had almost become a ritual for battle tactics to be subordinated to the needs of the knight. The commander would set out his battle formation with each unit protecting whilst displaying its respective banner as a matter of course. For it was deemed an honour for the knights to take up the forward positions in the battle formation as they were expected to win the day by their displays of chivalry in the ensuing fray. In successive engagements, particularly against the peasants, the Truchsess would deploy his light horse initially as a scouting party but also when swift manoeuvres were required during battle. However, there were two other reasons for the predilection for the deployment of horse. Generally, the mounted men-at-arms were deemed to be more reliable than their infantry counterparts. Moreover, the Truchsess could claim that a victory had been won without the need for any infantry deployment thereby saving the League having to pay out a victory bonus to his Landsknechts. This however backfired on a number of occasions, as at Leipheim and Königshofen, leading to mutinies within the rank and file.

1.4 The League Infantry

It is important to make a distinction between the two types of infantryman used by the League at this time. On the one hand were those paid foot soldiers commissioned by the members – Imperial cities, for example – many of whom would have served the defence of the city or their lord at some point. Here there would have prevailed some existing sense of loyalty. In addition, however, were those free-roaming mercenaries who owed only allegiance to a regular payment of their *Sold.* As matters would transpire, the key to building a formidable army in these times was discipline, but discipline had to be bought, so the 'business' of war and the availability of financial resources was to prove to be a major issue for the League during the campaigns of 1525.

Of the free-roaming mercenaries there were two initial pools of men which the League could draw on: the Swiss *Reisläufer* and the German *Landsknechte*. The term *Reislaufen* has been defined as 'the free decision taken by an individual to serve under a country, commander and/or flag of their choosing.'[28] This term became associated with those Swiss pikemen from the uplands who steadily built a reputation as some of the most effective fighting men on European soil. Since it was not financially or politically possible to maintain a standing professional army at this time, those needing to exert force to achieve their political aims were obliged to enlist the services of war lords or so-called *Kriegsherren*. These military contractors would in turn recruit men from all social classes who saw themselves as soldiers of fortune.

1.12. Bohemia had been a preferred source of mercenary infantry particularly during the latter half of the fifteenth century. Typically, these mercenaries were noted for their lack of body armour, preferring a leather doublet and the protection afforded by a pavise. Their main firearm was the crossbow which lost its effectiveness with the advent and deployment of the arquebus. Other notable weapons were the throwing axe and the *dusack* – a single-edged cutlass. The figure here is shown carrying an awl pike – a type of thrusting spear. Although the defeat of a Bohemian army during the Landshut War of Succession in 1504/5 had signalled their demise on the mercenary market, the poor supply of reliable footsoldiers forced the League to trawl more widely when recruiting for the 1525 campaign against the peasants.

The emergence of the term *Landsknecht* on German soil in the 1480s has been attributed to Peter von Hagenbach and was intended to indicate soldiers of the lowlands of Swabia as opposed to the 'upland' Swiss mercenaries. However, it was the Holy Roman Emperor Maximilian who formed the first mercenary Landsknecht regiments in 1487, later calling upon Georg von Frundsberg (1473–1528), to assist him in their organisation. As far as the Swiss were concerned, many were fighting in Northern Italy in the pay of Francis I, or being recruited by Duke Ulrich of Württemberg in his efforts to retake his duchy. As far as German Landsknechts were concerned, the League was at pains to find sufficient numbers at the time of the peasant uprising: the vast majority were absent with Georg von Frundsberg between October 1524 and March 1525, facing up to the Swiss and French in Northern Italy in the war between Charles V and Francis I which was to culminate in the Battle of Pavia.

Recruitment Issues

The recruitment of Landsknechts followed a fairly well-established procedure. Once the decision had been taken to engage in a war, a letter of commission (*Bestellungsbrief*) would be sent to a known military contractor. This would specify the number of men to recruit, the rates of pay, the date of commencement of the contract and clear orders relating to the command

28 Baumann (1994), p. 58.

structure. Since this was in effect a military contract it could be the subject of negotiation. At the end of January 1519 for instance, when the Swabian League mobilised for the first time against Duke Ulrich of Württemberg, the city of Augsburg took the lead in drawing up the letter of commission appointing Wilhelm Truchsess of Waldburg (the cousin of Georg) as the military contractor who in turn negotiated terms of the contract with the respected Landsknecht commander Burkhard von Ems. Von Ems was tasked with raising 1,000 men, and despite efforts by the city to keep their costs down, he was able to negotiate a monthly stipend of 30 florins plus four bodyguards and a page and an advanced payment of two florins for each recruit.[29]

The fixed rate for the services of Landsknecht, determined at the Imperial Diet at Constance in 1507, was four florins for a 30-day month (see Appendices II and III). This had to cover food, and wear and tear of clothing and equipment. It was not uncommon for additional supplements to be negotiated, particularly where mercenaries were in short supply and their market value was therefore higher. If a recruit brought suitable weapons and armour, then the value of this could be added to the wage. Some cities such as Augsburg paid an additional florin for equipment (*Rüstgulden*), others might issue rolls of cloth as payment, sometimes as a substitute for coin, sometimes as an additional incentive to those men keen on 'looking the part' (see Plates 2,3, 6 and 7). Nuremberg insisted on its men being clad in red – one of the only known attempts at 'uniform' during this period. Some cities also paid out an amount to cover the initial stand-down period (*Gartzeit*).

1.13. Landsknecht. This is perhaps a slightly more realistic depiction of a League foot soldier on campaign as many contemporary woodcuts would have us believe: hose torn at the knees, bonnet tied down around the chin and wearing a knotted 'poncho'. (Woodcut: Hans Schaufelein 1507)

One of the issues for the unattached mercenary who sought his fortune in any country which would pay was the denomination of the coin. For the Swabian League the coin of reference was the Rhineland florin which was the equivalent of 15 Batzen, which equalled 60 Kreuzer, which in turn amounted to 240 Pfennig or 480 Heller. Some returning Landsknechts from Italy may have brought with them 'Marcella' – half a Venetian *Lira*. Those mercenaries recruited from Northern Germany would have had the so-called *Schreckenberger* or *Stüber* coins in their purses.[30]

Compared to the occupations of the day, a mercenary was relatively well-paid, providing there was regular work. With impending unemployment, particularly as a battle neared its end, Landsknechts could expect a victory bonus, and there was an unwritten rule that

29 Baumann, op. cit., p. 51.
30 Baumann, p. 88.

1.14. Recruiting Landsknechts. (Woodcut: Pertracameister 'Von einemgesammelten Schatz', 1520)

they could plunder, extort and hold prisoners to ransom as 'extras'. This latter behaviour soon had to be regulated particularly since the League was at pains to secure funds for its ongoing costly campaign. Nevertheless, the prospect of booty was sometimes enough to lure men into the ranks who were not 'on the books'. Indeed when Georg von Frundsberg set out in 1526 for his Rome campaign he had what was known as the 'free company' (*Freifähnlein*) within his ranks.[31]

On 21 February von Eck consulted Georg von Waldburg and his recruiting officers Wolf Gremlich and Hans Freiberg about the chances of raising an army of 5,000 men. The League officials were of the view that this ought to be possible in parts of the Black Forest (still relatively peaceful at this point in time), Southern Tyrol and in the Palatinate and Hesse. Recruitment generally occurred using teams. A drummer and piper would mark their arrival and the promise of an advance of half a month's wage would be sufficient to garner interest from those men desperately in need of income and/or pure adventure. Those who turned up with weapons and armour – thereby saving the contractor additional expenses – would receive extra compensation. Others would be expected to buy their weapons at the place of muster. Recruits were generally drawn from rural and municipal labourers, although patricians might also turn up in the queue.[32]

31 *Ibid.*, pp. 86–91.
32 *Ibid.*, p. 64.

Box 1 Example of a city contingent from Biberach[33]

Example of a city contingent provided to the League by the Imperial city of Biberach for the Swabian Wars in 1499

100 men under the command of Konrad Starck (keeper of the Crown Inn)
2 *Doppelsöldner* – a patrician and a goldsmith – supplying their own body armour
19 men from Biberach
45 from the outlying villages
18 from villages for the sick (*Spitaldörfer*)
25 from villages outside of the municipal jurisdiction

Those who owned farmsteads tended not to succumb since they could not leave their livelihoods for any long period. Similarly, some of the towns were loath to entertain any recruitment activities, preferring to keep their own men for defensive duties. The Truchsess had some relatively rapid success in his own efforts, mobilising some 2,000 men in the Margraviate of Baden and in the Ortenau and Mertenau districts. However, he was required to take out a loan of 1,500 guilders to contribute to the cost. Wolf Gremlich on the other hand had little success. Reporting to Ulrich Artzt he complained that the vast majority of mercenaries in the upper territories were accompanied by their wives and children and he was at a loss as to how he was to meet their financial demands.[34] Gremlich's failure looked serious as at this juncture for there was still a shortfall of at least 2,000 of the projected force needed to march on Ulrich and to deal with the peasants. Fortunately for Gremlich, Wilhelm von Fürstenberg was able to come up with 2,000 foot which he had self-financed. On the strength of this von Fürstenberg was appointed commander of the League foot. By 10 March the number of infantry which had been mobilised numbered 4,000 – which amounted to four-fifths of the target figure. This was the force which was to march on Duke Ulrich. In the three weeks since the initial call to arms the peasant uprising had grown to such an extent that there were now serious questions concerning the loyalty of the League's troops – particularly those recruited from the Imperial cities. The League had to look further afield for its men and be flexible in its approach, looking to press-gang the peasants and any Swiss into service against Duke Ulrich in the first instance.

On 3 March Archduke Ferdinand wrote to the Truchsess:

> Our falconer's servant has returned from the field at Pavia with further news of victory over the king of France ... You should pass this news on wherever appropriate. We surmise that the Swiss will recall their soldiers who are rallying

33 <http://www.gfh-biberach.de/Hefte/BC-Heimatkundliche-Blätter-für-den-Kreis-Biberach/J23H1S04.pdf> (accessed 24 August 2018).

34 Quoted in Hoyer, p. 131.

> to duke Ulrich as soon as they hear the news from Italy, particularly since their soldiery has suffered considerable losses ... Therefore, we instruct you to proceed most energetically against such soldiers, Swiss or otherwise ... To this end, you should seek recruits under the terms of our public mandate from our rebellious subjects, the peasants in the Black Forest and elsewhere and hire them in the first instance to serve for a month at their own expense against our enemies the Swiss and others such as duke Ulrich who are invading our land. We shall in return forgive them the disfavour into which they have fallen with us, provided that they utterly abandon their disobedience and conduct themselves as loyal subjects. We have written in the same vein to our government in Ensisheim.[35]

Leonard von Eck, who was growing increasingly concerned about the commitment of sections of the League foot, suggested to Duke Wilhelm of Bavaria to recruit further afield, particularly Bohemia. This was undertaken with limited success as far as the League was concerned although somewhat belatedly and at greater expense than normal.[36]

From April onwards, the League was finally able to draw on the services of those Landsknechts from Northern Italy who were returning from their victory in Pavia. By the middle of the month the first contingent of 1,200 men had been noted by Ulrich Artzt as being men 'ready to serve anybody'.[37] This was not always the case, however. When Archduke Ferdinand sought to recruit those men under the command of Marx Sittich von Ems, who had fought in Milan, they 'refused to allow themselves be recruited against the peasants and dispersed to their homes once they had been paid.'[38]

Truchsess Georg adopted a more nuanced approach. Based on his experience, the best troops who had fought under him came from the Hegau region and the Black Forest. However, these were areas affected by the uprising. Realising this difficulty, as the campaign against the peasants unfolded he directed his attention further south towards the area bordering Lake Constance and specifically those Landsknechts who had allied with the peasants of the Lake band. Having neutralised the peasant threat via a peace treaty at Weingarten, the Truchsess targeted those Landsknechts from their

1.15. *Feldwebel* – responsible for organising the infantry into battle formation. (Woodcut: Erhard Schön)

35 Scott and Scribner, pp. 152–3.

36 Johann Edmund Jörg, 1851 *Deutschland in der Revolutionsperiode von 1522 bis 1526* (Freiburg in Breisgau: Herdersche Buchandlungsverlag, 1851), quoted in Hoyer, op. cit., p. 131.

37 Vogt, pp. 233, 261.

38 Letter to Duke Wilhelm of Bavaria, quoted in Jörg, p. 241.

ranks who would be at a loose end. By recruiting these men, he would show to the peasants that they would not be able to put their faith in these mercenaries in future. Should there be a risk, von Waldburg had plans to deploy these units further afield where their loyalties to the peasant cause would be weaker.[39]

Box 2: The Muster[40]

The main purpose of the muster was to engender a sense of loyalty to the cause of the regiment by extracting an oath of allegiance to the supreme commander, his officers and the cause. From a later woodcut in Leonard Fronsberger's *Kriegsbuch* dated 1565, we can surmise that new recruits would have been expected to walk through an arch created by two halberds and a pike crosspiece as a symbol of acceptance of the code. To the side would be sitting a scribe who would note down the name and available weaponry. Interestingly, a similar *Spiessjoch*, as it was known, was used by the peasants falling under the jurisdiction of the Abbey of Kempten in 1523 to pledge their resistance to the princes. The muster would often be overseen by officials of the contracting party – not the commander – as it was not uncommon for corrupt practices such as double counting or 'ghosting' to occur to inflate the ranks and therefore the amount which would have to be billed to the authorities. At the muster, the rules of engagement laid down in the so-called *Artikelsbrief* would be read out. The first record of such articles of war dates from 1519 when the League mobilised against Duke Ulrich, and they covered discipline, rules of engagement, and representational rights of the infantryman. The final act at the muster would be the swearing of an oath at which each Landsknecht was expected to remove his headgear.

The Muster

Once recruited, the new League infantryman was expected to turn up at an appointed place for the muster (*Musterung*). They might be paid two florins (*Laufgeld*) in advance to cover the cost between recruitment and acceptance into the ranks. We know that most recruits were requested to muster near Ulm – the League's headquarters. However, regular musters were required as the campaign unfolded in order to take stock of the available men and weaponry and to announce new and old regulations and rules of engagement. Following the suppression of the peasants in Franconia the Truchsess returned to Ulm where stock was taken. July invoices submitted by the company commanders reveal troop reductions. So, for example, Wolf Pfaffenlapp's company had lost 38 men down from 400 in April. Wendel von Weier's troop had been depleted by 57 – down from 436. Wolf Wurmser's company had seen a drop of 73 men down

39 Vogt, p. 294.

40 R. Baumann, *Landsknechte* (1994), C.H. Beck, pp. 48–72. Translation: author.

from 437. Kaspar von Rothenhan had 361 men remaining against an April muster of 422.[41] We do not know which proportions of these figures were casualties, desertions or mercenaries who had left the ranks having earned sufficient through plunder.

1.5 The League Ordnance

The consensus at the time in the League Council was that heavy artillery would not be necessary for a campaign against the peasants but that lighter cannon would be required,[42] and for every contingent of 300 foot soldiers provided by a League member, there was an expectation that these troops were to be accompanied at the very least by a light field piece – a culverin or falconet.

1.16. Landsknecht swearing-in ceremony. Note that the men have removed their headgear for this and have raised two fingers to take the oath. (Woodcut from Thomas Murner-'Grosser lutherischer Narr', 1522. Artist unknown)

1.17. Michael Ott von Echterdingen (1479–1532) was awarded the office of Master General of the Ordnance (*ObersterZeugmeister*) in 1501 by the Emperor Maximilian (himself a patron of all matters relating to artillery). Von Echterdingen had proved himself during the Italian Wars between 1507 and 1510 as well as in the conflict with the Duke of Württemberg. He was a known military theorist and widely regarded as 'the first modern artillerist of German history', and took command of the artillery in the army of the Swabian League. This portrait medallion was minted on the occasion of his 43rd birthday in 1522.

41 Blickle, p. 272.
42 Hoyer, p. 115.

The German word for the term culverin – *Feldschlange* – first appeared around 1440 and originates probably from the decorative work applied to the barrel or the muzzle to make the cannon look like a snake or dragon. Culverins had a smaller calibre than cannon (*Hauptbüchse*, used for siege work), with larger pieces having a 13 cm bore. Small lighter versions of a culverin with a calibre down to 5 cm were generally referred to as a falconet (*Falkonett*) and smaller still (3.5 cm) a serpentine (*Serpentinell*).[43] Field artillery pieces generally had a longer barrel to calibre ratio providing greater range, accuracy and force and would normally be pulled by one or two horses to maintain flexibility and mobility in battle. As we shall see these were to prove crucial against the peasants.

The Emperor Maximilian (1459–1519) had taken great interest in artillery and the science of ballistics and had an inventory recorded of his entire arsenal in Innsbruck.[44] During the late medieval period artillery had been developing away from siege ordnance to lighter, longer field pieces. However, this had been occurring in a quite haphazard way and the Emperor needed to establish an overview and system for classifying the contents of his arsenal. His system of classification was based on the weight of the (usually iron) cannonball.

Table 3. Types of Ordnance

Type	Description	Weight of cannonball
Hauptbüchsen	Heavy siege cannon – barrel carried on a wagon	40–50 kg
Scharfmetzen	Lighter siege gun on a wheeled carriage	25–35 kg
Kartaunen	German adoption of the Italian word 'quartana bombarda'- its cannonball was one quarter of the weight of a siege cannonball.	12–25 kg
Basilisken	Field artillery piece with a longerbarrel	8–12 kg

His successor Charles V would eventually change to a calibre-based classification by the middle of the century, to reflect the many different types of artillery pieces which were subsequently being developed.[45] The *Kartaune*, for example, would receive further fractional sub-classifications based on calibre. What is clear, even from the Innsbruck inventory, is that field artillery – that is, barrels mounted on carriages (*Lafetten*) of all lengths and calibres – were already in development. Although the League had requisitioned light ordnance from its members as the war progressed and more and more field pieces were captured from the peasants, the types of available artillery would

43 Master gunners christened their bronze casts with the names of birds and mythical animals such as Robinet, Falcon(et), Serpentine, Culverine (a grass snake).

44 *Zeugbuch Kaiser Maximilians I* (Maximilian's Book of Artillery) – Bayerische Staatsbibliothek München Clm 222, fol. 19r resp. 58r. The whole catalogue is available for viewing online under the identifier BSB Cod.icon. 222 at the Munich DigitalisierungsZentrum.

45 For a classification of artillery and their ranges, cf. Thomas Arnold, *The Renaissance at War* (London: Cassell, 2001), pp. 30–31.

have varied, particularly since the rebels had liberated cannon from the many castles they had successfully stormed.

Artillery was generally provided by the Imperial Cities since it was here that both the technology and the necessary expertise existed to cast bronze cannon. *Buechsenmeisterei* or 'matters of ordnance' as it came to be known was considered to be a great science and a master gunner had to read, write, possess scientific knowledge about the properties of gunpowder and the relationship between calibre and trajectory and above all be prepared to experiment. As knowledge expanded, this was captured in handwritten manuscripts and/or passed on orally from master to apprentice. Until the publication of *von den probierten Künsten* in 1535 by Franz Helm, the main reference works were the 'Book of Pyrotechnics' (*Das Feuerwerksbuch*) of 1420 (published as *Büchsenmeisterei*' in 1529), and *Das buch der stryt vnd buchßen*' written by Philipp Mönch in 1496). Most knowledge was understandably preciously guarded and the so-called *Büchsenmeister* or master gunners – a highly esteemed profession – were often charged with the responsibility of maintaining the municipal arsenal. The master gunner's expertise encompassed not only the ability to cast cannon – usually in bronze procured from church bells – he also had to be adept at the newly evolving science of ballistics. This new knowledge was highly valuable and secretly guarded thus giving the gunnery master considerable wealth and esteem. Casting bronze cannon had made enormous strides by the early sixteenth century through the development of better furnaces and the discovery of new tougher bronze alloys which reduced weight and therefore cost.

If a city made artillery available for a campaign, master gunners would command a hefty price since the profession was a dangerous one. Artillery at this time was still in its infancy and imperfectly cast cannon could burst during firing, or there might be accidents with gunpowder. In battle, gunners who had not been trained to defend themselves in hand-to-hand combat were highly vulnerable although they were more than likely to be taken prisoner for their ability and knowledge. Since master gunners were holders of a particular form of military intelligence, they could easily be poached and accused of treachery.[46] Consequently they were highly prized and found themselves at the centre of disputes between the League and its members. Thus, when the League Council made a request to the city of Augsburg for a further four field pieces with powder, shot and equipment and that these should be manned by several gunners' mates paid at twice the rate of a rank-and-file mercenary, i.e. *Doppelsold* – the city's request was denied.[47] These difficulties in raising the necessary ordnance and requisite support were by no means rare. Municipalities could be cleaned out of their skilled tradesmen for periods at a time, since alongside the craft of the master gunner an army would need the expertise of wheelwrights, blacksmiths,

46 Rainer Leng, 'Gründe für berufliches Töten, Büchsenmeister und Kriegshauptleute zwischen Berufsethos und Gewissensnot', in Horst Brunner (ed.), *Der Krieg im Mittelalter und in der Frühen Neuzeit: Gründe, Begründungen, Bilder, Recht* (Imagines Medii Aevi. Interdisziplinäre Beiträge zur Mittelalterforschung, band 3; Wiesbaden 1999), pp. 307–348.

47 *Ibid.*

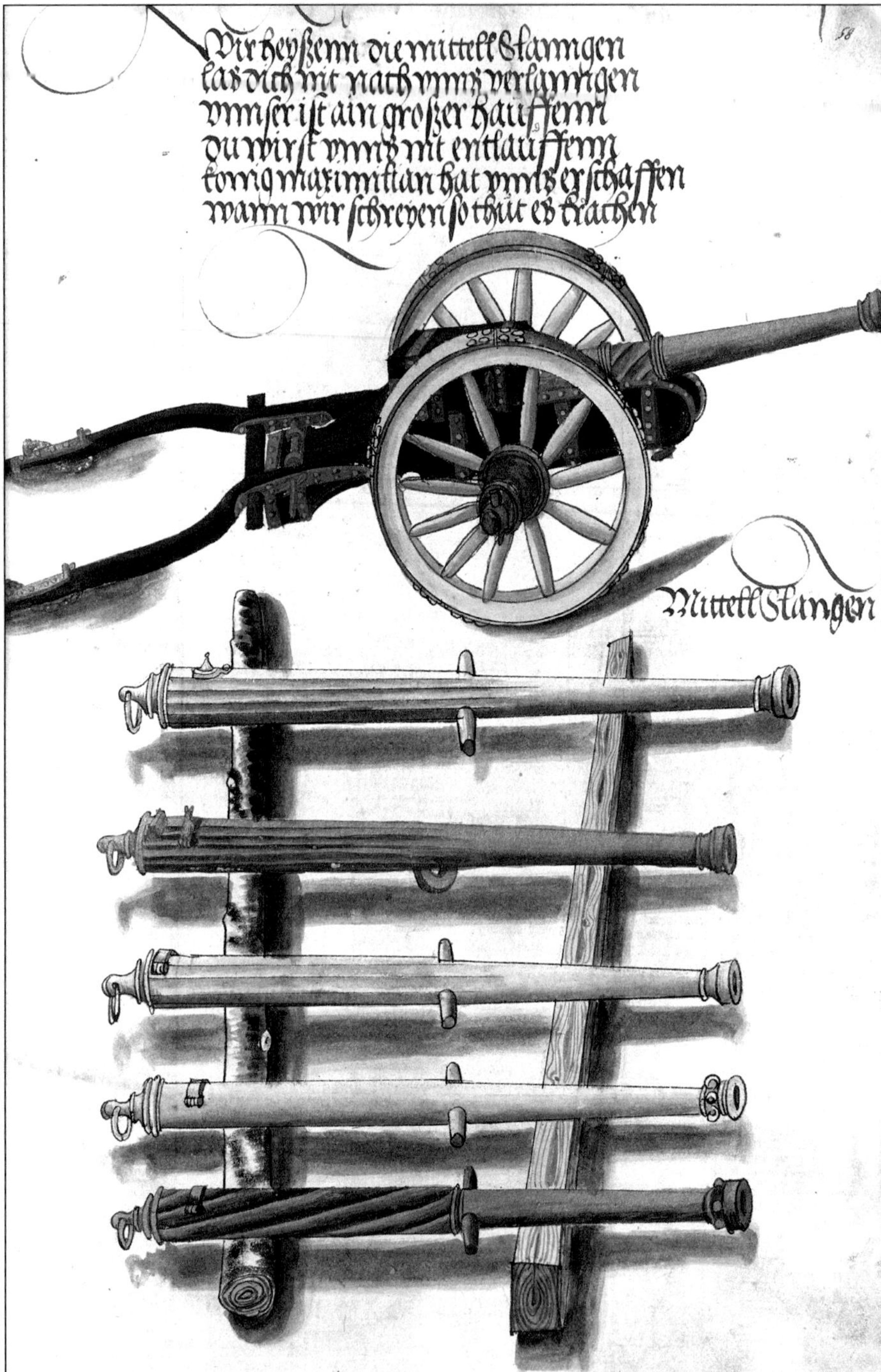

1.18. This coloured drawing from a whole series cataloguing the Imperial arsenal inventory at Innsbruck was painted by Bartholomaeus Freysleben. It depicts a falconet and a selection of barrels. By attaching a frame to the gun carriage, the gun could easily be moved by a single horse. This was in fact a forerunner of the so-called 'galloper gun'. A lighter field piece (falconet/culverin) had a much more violent recoil than the heavier cannon (*Kartaune*) and would have almost leapt into the air on discharge. Some form of restraint – ropes or digging in the trail – may have been required when in action. Such mobile falconets could be deployed swiftly. This inventory item also shows a number of differently shaped barrels which suggest that these were either used interchangeably or were waiting for their own carriage. 'Zeugbuch Kaiser Maximilians I' (Maximilian's Book of Artillery). (München Zeugbuch Kaiser Maximilians I. – BSB Cod. icon. 222, Innsbruck, um 1502. Courtesy: Bayerische Staatsbibliothek)

leatherworkers, masons, basket weavers, carpenters, tailors, cobblers, and last but not least armourers. Nevertheless, by the time the League army was engaging with the peasants of Upper Swabia, as at the Battle of Wurzach for example, the Truchsess had 18 artillery pieces at his disposal, four of which had been taken following the rout of the peasants at Leipheim. From invoices historians have been able to piece together the initial size of the complement which accompanied the League ordnance. Each artillery piece had its own assigned master gunner. In addition there were four carpenters, three sappers (*Schneller*), and for each gun a blacksmith (*Schlosser*) and two gunner's mates, the latter both responsible for the gunpowder. Each master gunner or bombardier had between two and six assistants and depending on the size of the artillery piece would need carters to manage the required number of horses. In May the League had 91 draught horses but by June that number had expanded to 208 with a complement of 42 contracted carters and 69 drovers.[48]

During encampment, the artillery park would most probably have been kept separate. We can surmise this from at least two sources. In 1444 Emperor Friedrich III decreed that the entire German and Austrian artillery were to enjoy certain rights and responsibilities which was to set them apart from the rest of the train.[49] We know that this special status still existed beyond the time of the Peasants' War from a woodcut by Jost Amman, which dates much later, from the middle of the sixteenth century, and depicts the artillery camp as a separate entity existing within the massive wagon fort of the Imperial army. Under the letter of articles,[50] gunners were permitted to ride on the munition wagons apart from the main baggage train, and house their families in the artillery park as they were generally expected to camp near their cannon.[51] Guarding the artillery was a matter of honour for a Landsknecht.

By the end of the campaign, as the League army acquired the artillery pieces discarded by the peasants, the gun train must have been enormous, particularly when one considers the supply wagons necessary to sustain such ordnance, which required sturdier versions to carry powder and shot and then basic equipment for earthworks. Inventories at the turn of the century give us an idea of the type of equipment: ladders, wicker lattices for making earthworks, boards to hang over the side of the wagon for added protection, 4 metres of chain, rope, shovels, pickaxes, mattocks (hoes), pans, two axes, short

48 Blickle, p. 151, based on invoices from Hans Dietl (Artillery officer – *Feldzeugmeister*), Hans Felber (Master Gunner – *Büchsenmeister*), and Konrad Stuber (head carter – *Geschirrmeister*) dated June 1525. City archives, Augsburg.

49 Letter of Articles issued in 1444 by Emperor Friedrich III to the entire German and Austrian artillery concerning their privileges (*Artikelbrief des Kaiser Friedrich III an die gesamte deutsche und österreichische Arkelley aus dem Jahre 1444 über deren Privilegien* (Freyheiten und Gerechtigkeiten für al Zeyt), quoted in Anton Dolleczek 1887, *Geschichte der österreichischen Artillerie*, quoted in Dolleczek, *Geschichte der österreichischen Artillerie*, Vienna, 1887). These lasted well into the 19th century.

50 Cf. in Leonard Fronsberger's 1575 treatise, *The Book of War* (*Kriegsbuch*) available at <https://reader.digitale-sammlungen.de/en/fs1/object/display/bsb10989917_00001.html>.

51 *Ibid.*

1.19. Baggage Train and Trossweibel. (Woodcut: Erhard Schon)

wooden blocks, staves, sickles and a scythe and a log the length of the wagon.[52] Contemporary accounts of Duke Ulrich of Württemberg's artillery train give us an idea of the size of tail of an army on the march – even before the baggage train is allowed for. The Duke expected the monastery and municipalities in his territory to provide a total of 378 supply wagons which were designated to specific pieces of artillery in his train. If one estimates four horses or oxen per wagon length, 1,512 draught animals were required. Allowing for 10 metres per wagon length, this could generate an enormous tail![53]

1.6 The Baggage Train

At the Imperial Diet in Constance in 1507 military contractors were absolved from the responsibility of providing equipment, food and shelter for their troops as long as they kept paying them. This was laid down in a detailed

52 LeoVogt, 1504, *Die Chronik des Georg Schwarzerdt* (Ubstadt-Weiher:Verlag Regionalkultur, 2000), p. 75.

53 Klaus Huss, Herrmann Füllbert, *Das württembergische Heer vor Bretten 1504* <https://www.landsknechte-bretten.de/wissenswertes/das-wurttembergische-heer-vor-bretten–1504/> (accessed 25 October 2018).

schedule entitled *Sold, Kost und Schaden* (pay, maintenance and damages). The common foot soldier was thus expected to provide his own weapons and equipment and meet all necessary outlays from his pay. Everything which a fighting soldier required was available: food, weapons, medical attention and recreation. Estimates of daily individual consumption during the first quarter of the sixteenth century cover 750 g of bread, 500 g of meat, two litres of beer (generally seen as a principal form of nutrition) or wine, and 100 g each of smoked ham, butter and cheese. Since many Landsknechts had their families in train the demand would multiply.

This more than anything accounts for the enormous baggage train or *Tross* which trundled its way across the countryside behind an army on the march in the early modern era. When one considers a ratio of 1:1 for an army to its camp followers, then the Swabian League army would have resembled an enormous juggernaut as it wound its way through much of southern Germany during the first half of 1525.

With an average complement of 1,500 horse and 6,000 foot, the logistical challenge to supply the League army during a six-month campaign was enormous. This task fell to the appointed quartermasters, Wilhelm von Baldeck and then his replacement Heinrich Treusch von Beutler. The *Quartiermeister* was an important senior rank in the supreme command group, with a responsibility for locating and preparing locations for the army's encampment, oversight of the camp market and the traders and the camp of the baggage train. Given the size of his task he worked closely together with the provost (*Profoss*), who was responsible for maintaining discipline.

1.20. Provost. (Woodcut: Erhard Schön)

One of the first items to be erected – usually in the centre of the camp – was a gallows. This served to remind camp followers that they were indeed bound by the strict codes laid down in the army field ordinance. The role of the provost was to police the camp market, to supervise the correct use of weights and measures and maintain agreed opening times and prices on specific goods. Needless to say, the opportunity to tax the traders meant that this could be a lucrative office. To assist the provost in the prosecution of camp law and to punish the enemy, the League appointed Berthold Aichelin as executioner. He joined the army from Ulm after the Battle of Leipheim.[54]

54 Aichelin was the League official executioner although he carried the title of provost. *Blätter für Wuerttembergische Kirchengeschichte* 1892, Vol. 7, No. 4. *Berthold*

1.21. This image from the siege of Münster 1535 shows a quite elaborate camp kitchen centred around one or more large cauldrons, but also including smaller pots standing by the fire or pans managed by individual cooks. The English term 'sutler' derives from the German word 'sud' which describes the broth which (apart from beer) would have been the basic form of sustenance of the day. (Artist: Erhard Schön)

Further officers under the command of the *Quartiermeister* were the commissary (*Proviantmeister*) who coordinated supplies, and the master at arms (*Wachtmeister*) who was generally responsible for camp security. The quartermaster also commanded the company fouriers. The baggage train itself had its own officer – the so-called *Trossweibel* – often called the *Hurenweibel* (sergeant of the whores) whose task it was to keep order both within the baggage train and within its camp. This would prove to be no mean feat.

Ensuring that vast array of wagons carts and pack animals arrived and departed in an orderly manner, particularly in inclement weather, was a regular challenge, particularly since the Tross had to be kept separate from the army on the march. Contemporary images show the train strewn across the landscape as the many traders would no doubt have vied to arrive in good time to get the best pitches in the market. Given the disposable income of the average mercenary foot soldier, the commercial prospects which the *Tross* offered to sutlers, butchers, bakers, pedlars and of course prostitutes, acted like a magnet for prospective traders and their assistants. Such a market, however, required both organisation and discipline and traders would require often written permission to sell their wares as well as abide those rules as laid down in the army's field ordinance.

Aichelin der Bundesprofoss <https://www.deutsche-digitale-bibliothek.de/item/X3E2LCX5TLL3DI7DWDU6V7UIKB22DGWQ> (accessed 23 November 2018).

1.22. Supply Wagons. Campaigns required vast amounts of supplies. This extract from the Triumph of Maximilian shows supply wagons carrying pikes and a collapsible windlass for hoisting cannon barrels on to their carriages or into position in siegeworks. The artillery here are in black and red imperial livery. It is unlikely that the League ordnance bore any distinct colour scheme as ordnance was on loan from a number of cities an/or captured during the campaigns. The two falconets to the right have been rendered mobile by the addition of a wooden-framed harness with each being drawn by a single horse. (Courtesy: Biblioteca Digital Hispanica)

Box 3: Hans Sachs Poem in Column of Mercenaries Woodcut.

Here we follow with cheerful spirits;
Early this morning the scouts went off
To prepare a camp for us tonight
As soon as we have beaten the enemy
We will stay there overnight
The wagons will be drawn in a circle,
And the master of the watch and the quartermaster
Are waiting for the army there[55]

The campaigns required vast amounts of supplies. In Württemberg alone between 1515 and 1520 municipalities and monasteries were expected to provide Duke Ulrich. It was usually left to the cities to provide the wagons for the train and they often carried a pennant fore and aft on the ridge of canopy bearing the municipal coat of arms, as the illustration in Plate 8 shows.

1.7 The League's Communications

The military superiority of the League owed no small debt to three key facets of its information war: an effective system of communication, a propaganda effort and a spy network. In this digital age it is easy to forget that military communications at this time were heavily dependent on despatch riders. By 1525 the Imperial cities had in place a relatively well-oiled despatch system. The League secretariat based in Ulm made extensive use of this service. Despatch riders were already organised into an association which

55 Text to a woodcut by Erhard Schon entitled Column of Mercenaries by Hans Sachs in Keith Moxey, *Peasants Warriors and Wives* (Chicago: Chicago Press, 1989) p.80

facilitated a coordination of this mail service. Whilst Ulm acted as the communications nerve centre, the city of Augsburg also played a central role as the correspondence of Ulrich Artzt the Augsburg official who also acted as the cities' representative within the League demonstrates.[56] The League was quick to spread news of threats and successes in its campaign against Duke Ulrich and the peasants. Not only was there a great acceleration in correspondence during the middle of 1525, there was also a stepping up of the publication of pamphlets with the League making use of the printing facilities in Augsburg to disseminate their anti-peasant propaganda. Examples of such publications include the exclusion notice served on the three Upper Swabian peasant bands dated 16 March, charging the same with a gross breach of territorial peace within the Holy Roman Empire and the neglect of their oaths and obligations vis-à-vis their lords. More publications followed on 14 April detailing conditions of surrender of the Leipheim rebels; the unwillingness of the peasants to negotiate terms with the authorities; accusations of iconoclasm on the part of the rebels; notification of the terms of the Treaty of Weingarten; the defeat of the rebels at Herrenberg/Böblingen; a 9 May proclamation to condemn revolutionaries to death, repeated on 10 and 12 June; and single-leaf woodcuts detailing the names of castles and priories which had been attacked by the peasants in the Black Forest, Swabia and Franconia.[57] Some of the propaganda was posted in prominent public places and read out for those who were illiterate. The absence of the means to mount a public counter-propaganda effort on the part of the rebels made it difficult to swim against the tide of public opinion.

In addition to the League's propaganda effort, it was vital to have as much intelligence as possible about the peasants' movements. The Truchsess employed spies wherever possible, as at Wurzach, Gaisbeuren and Weingarten. The positions of the Allgäu peasants were also known prior to commencement of action at Leubas.[58] We can surmise that similar subterfuge was used at other key points during the campaign. It would not have been difficult to extort collaboration from peasants under threat of punishment or a fire avoidance tax. Some historians have charged certain peasant leaders with having been turned, as at Leubas, for example.[59]

---

56 Wolfgang Wüst, 'Kommunikation und Bündnis – Zur Rolle oberdeutscher Reichstädte', in Elmar Kuhn, *Der Bauernkrieg in Oberschwaben* (Tübingen: Bibliotheca Academica Verlag, 2000), p. 449.

57 Blickle, pp. 310–3.

58 *Ibid.*, p. 308.

59 Trauchburg, pp. 189–92.

Part II

The Campaigns

2.1. The League's Campaign against Duke Ulrich of Württemberg

As we have seen, the exiled Duke of Württemberg continued to remain a thorn in the side of the League in his determination to retake his duchy. Symbolically this meant his city of residence – Stuttgart. In 1524 after five years of exile the time now seemed ripe – the peasants and municipalities, particularly in the territories owned by the Archduke Ferdinand, were becoming openly defiant and therefore not only a matter of concern for the House of Habsburg but also the League. Moreover, the inhabitants of Württemberg for the most part, detested the house of Austria, and, despite his exactions and oppression in the past, still retained a degree of feudal-patriotic affection for their duke.

In September 1524 the Princes' commissioners at Engen reported to the Austrian officials in Innsbruck:

> As you have instructed us to ascertain his [Ulrich's] and other insurrectionists' intentions … and, should he be planning a war or rising, … we beg to inform you … that up to now as many as five hundred horse and infantry have made their way by stealth night and day to Hohentwiel, and are growing more each day. He has also brought considerable provisions thither. Over and above that he has a foundryman who has cast all the copper …; his mounted scouts are ranging throughout the Hegau … He is stirring among the peasantry to hand it over to his control. We suspect and surmise – inasmuch as reports have reached us – that the peasants throughout the Hegau have formed a secret conspiracy and pact among themselves – that they are planning to rebel and to refuse their lords rents and service, to which they mean to agree on 2 October [when they have all foregathered] in a village called Hilzingen, close by Hohentwiel, at its church [festival] that day. They plan to form a league around which he [Ulrich] can rally them, to which end he is already negotiating today, in order to attack his princely grace's villages and the territory of Württemberg and to start a war.[1]

1 Scott and Scribner, pp. 49–150.

On the request of Archduke Ferdinand, the six appointed councillors and the three members of the executive held an emergency meeting in Ulm on 8 January 1525 having received letters about the disturbances in his county of Nellenburg, and peasant actions in the Hegau, the Black Forest, the town of Villingen, and other subjects of the Archduke's territory. The Council was of the view that since the disparate peasant bands had not yet united, largely because of the weather, the League needed to engage in a pre-emptive strike. However, the majority of troops were in Italy at this time so it was a decided that the League assembly scheduled for March should be brought forward to February to determine the mobilisation of a rapid action force (*Eilende Hilfe*).

Dr Johannes Schad, the Habsburg representative on the Princes' bench, was the most vociferous in demanding the deployment of the rapid action force to meet the triple threat of the peasants of Stühlingen, the rebellious citizens of Waldshut and the actions of Duke Ulrich. The rapid action force had been proscribed at a fifth of the total League complement – 369 mounted men-at-arms and 2,167 infantry.[2] The situation seemed to be deteriorating when news reached Ulm that Ulrich had ordered heavy cannon to be brought from Zurich and Solothurn to the fortress at Hohentwiel and was openly recruiting disaffected peasants and Swiss mercenaries.

Ulrich promised the Swiss *Reisläufer* a monthly wage of five and a half florins to join his campaign. By February 1525, in addition to the steadily growing Swiss presence in his ranks there was now an ever-expanding peasant contingent largely made up of men from the Hegau and Klettgau regions. By contrast Georg von Waldburg, whom the Archduke had appointed as his supreme commander, was slowly running out of the finances needed to keep his army in the field. The Archduke swiftly responded by drawing on the financial might of the Fugger family. The Fuggers, along with the

2.1.1. Hohentwiel is an extinct volcano in the Hegau region of Baden-Württemberg in southern Germany, which lies to west of the city of Singen and 20 miles (30 km) from Lake Constance. In 1521, it was passed on to Duke Ulrich von Württemberg, who developed Hohentwiel into one of the strongest fortresses in the territory. From here he launched his unsuccessful campaign to retake his duchy. (Photo: Peter Stein)

2 Blickle, p. 110.

Welser family based in Augsburg, were venture capitalists and international mercantile bankers who controlled much of the European economy at this time. Their close affiliation with the House of Habsburg had enable the latter's rise to European domination.

On 11 February the League, mindful of the growing double threat, stepped up their military commitment and authorised the first 'third' of the League's overall contingent – the equivalent of 600 horse and 3,500 infantry. They were to muster at Ulm within two weeks. Greater emphasis, however, was placed on the raising of horse rather than foot as the consensus within the League was that infantry could not be trusted.[3] Debate ensued regarding the release of a second 'third' – the delegates from Mainz and the Palatinate at this point still preferring to negotiate – but as reports continued to paint a deteriorating picture, the second third was then approved. It would of course take time for this recruitment and mobilisation to be undertaken, and time was running out as news arrived that the Duke had left his fortress at Hohentwiel on 23 February. It was no secret that Ulrich had been in the service of Francis I since 1521, and the King is said to have given him his blessing from Pavia since this was in effect a strike against the Habsburgs on home soil.

2.1.2.a. & b. The Duke of Württemberg's armour commissioned for his personal use in an earlier military expedition in Italy and the anticipated triumphal procession in Rome. Wrought by Wilhelm von Worms the Elder, the leading armourer of Nuremberg, it is adorned in gold with figures of noblewomen, the Duke's motto, and a spectacular dragon. (Courtesy: Philadelphia Museum of Art)

3 Blickle, p. 111.

When Ulrich began his campaign, estimates of an army of 6,000 Landsknechts in 13 companies and 300 mounted men-at-arms were reported to the League but the numbers were disputed as being too low. Ulrich Artzt put these at 10,000 and 800 respectively, figures with which Georg von Waldburg concurred. What was less well understood was the size of the peasant bands which were joining the Duke. As the Duke himself expressed it, he was determined to come to his rights, 'if not by the aid of the spur, by that of the shoe', by which was meant, of course, that on the failure of the negotiations he was making with the knights and nobles of various districts, extending even to Bohemia, he was prepared to enter into a league with the rebellious peasants.[4] Hans Müller von Bulgenbach, a well-respected Landsknecht who had served in France, commanded a large band of peasants originating from the Black Forest and began spreading out through the districts of Klettgau and the Hegau to the west of Lake Constance. He had joined Ulrich's ranks. Ulrich also pinned his hopes on elements of the Württemberg militia, which at a muster in 1524 had counted 5,828 pike, 1,903 handgunners, and 1,188 halberdiers.[5] Ulrich had considerable heavy ordnance in his train. From inventories it is known that he had at least two heavy siege cannon, (*Kartaunen*) each capable of firing 40 lb shot, and two lighter culverins firing between six and 24 lb cannonballs. These required 115 wagons and 16 tons of gunpowder.[6]

At this point in time Georg von Waldburg could not match Duke Ulrich's complement. He hurriedly recruited 2,000 men in late February and they mustered in four companies in Wolfach on 8 March. His cousin promised him a further 4,000 men from Württemberg. As 4,753 florins arrived from the League, his captains were able to order 700 pikes as well as lead shot and powder for the handgunners. The Austrian contingent of horse proved to be easier to assemble and numbered 452 for the whole campaign (see Appendix IV).

Ulrich marched north from Hohentwiel to Tuttlingen pursued by the Truchsess. The first encounter took place at Balingen, some 35 km to the south of Tübingen, where the League's troops defeated units of Hegau and Black Forest peasants in the pay of the Duke and took their standard. Ulrich pressed onwards having attempted to take the town, but it refused to swear him allegiance. He left his heavy cannon in haste.[7] When a similar refusal was forthcoming at Rosenfeld, it looked as though Ulrich's hopes of raising of Württemberg militias was not going to transpire as he had thought.

As Ulrich continued his march on Stuttgart he received some unwelcome news. Francis I had been defeated and taken prisoner at the Battle of Pavia. Some 5,000 Swiss *Reisläufer* were included in the 12,000 casualties. News spread like wildfire and it had an immediate effect on the Swiss recruits in

---

4 Belfort Bax, <https://www.marxists.org/archive/bax/1899/peasants-war/ch02.htm#n3> (accessed 29 August 18).

5 L.J. Stadlinger, *Geschichte des württembergischen Kriegswesens von der frühesten bis zur neuesten Zeit* (Stuttgart:1856), quoted in Blickle, p. 114.

6 *Ibid.*

7 It is not clear from the German whether this was a single piece or several.

Plate 1 Command Group of the Swabian League army. Illustration by and © Geoff Laws 2019. See Colour Plate Commentaries for further information.

A

B

C

D

Plate 2 Swabian League banners.
See Colour Plate Commentaries for further information.

A

B

C

D

Plate 3 Swabian League banners.
See Colour Plate Commentaries for further information.

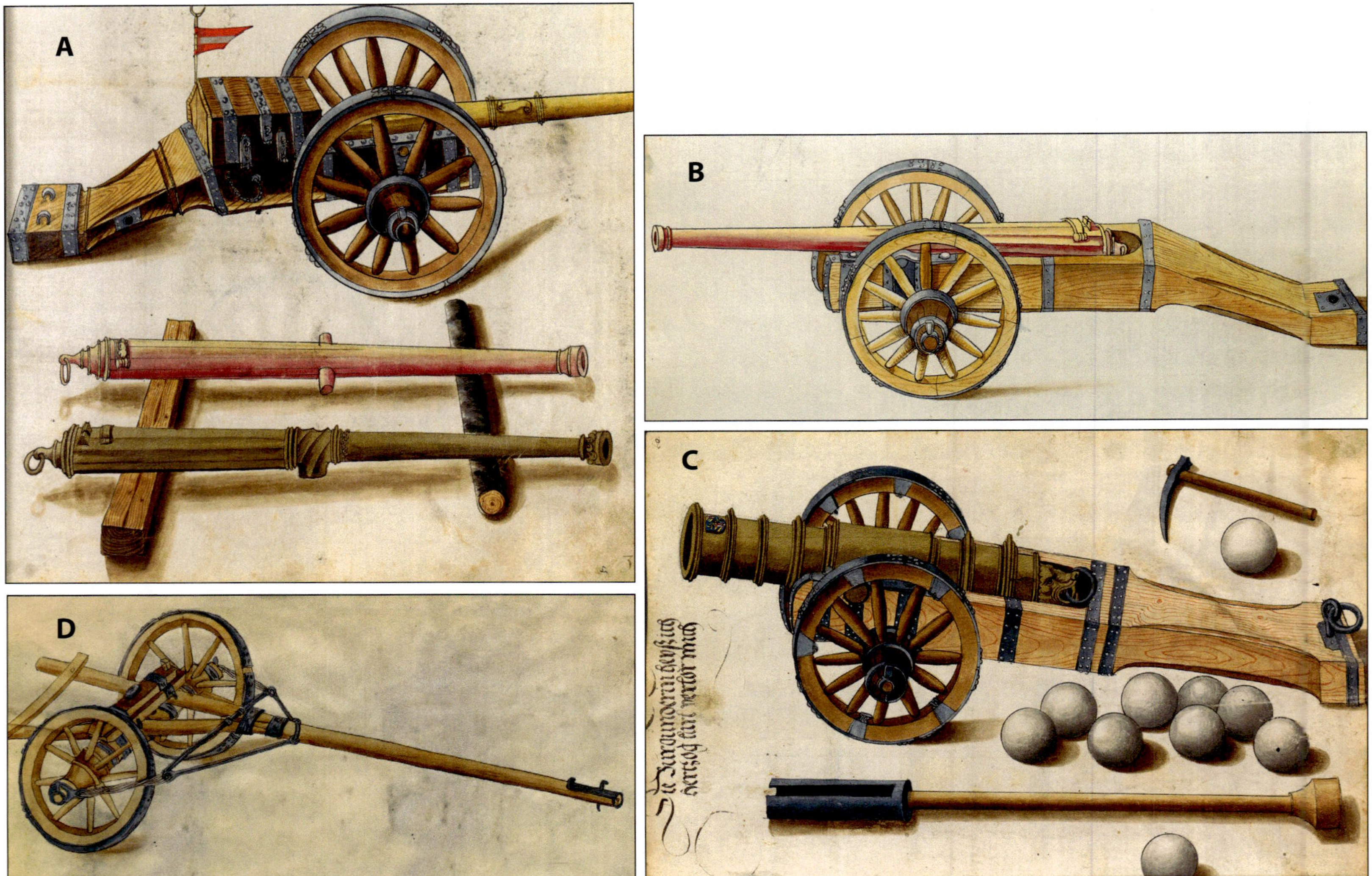

Plate 4 Ordnance. See Colour Plate Commentaries for further information.

Plate 5 League light horse**.**
See Colour Plate Commentaries
for further information.

Plates 6 Swabian League banners.
See Colour Plate Commentaries for further information.

Plate 7 Swabian League banners.
See Colour Plate Commentaries for further information.

A

B

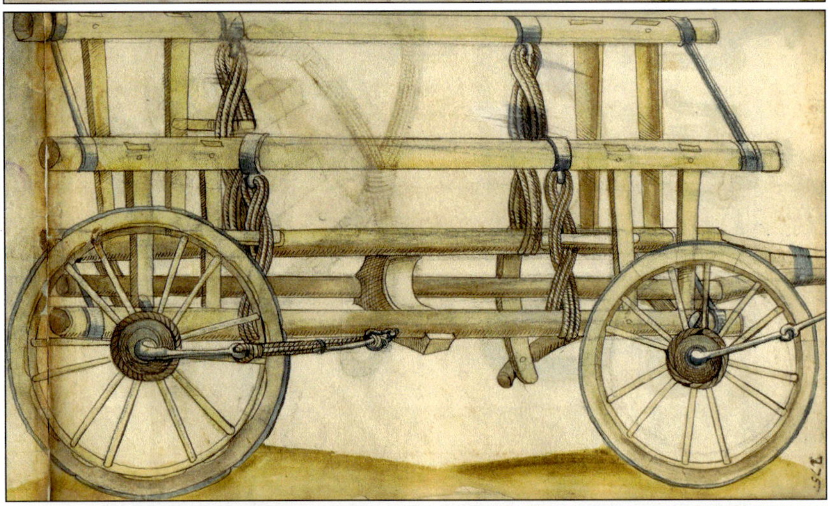

C

Plate 8 Baggage and Artillery Trains. See Colour Plate Commentaries for further information.

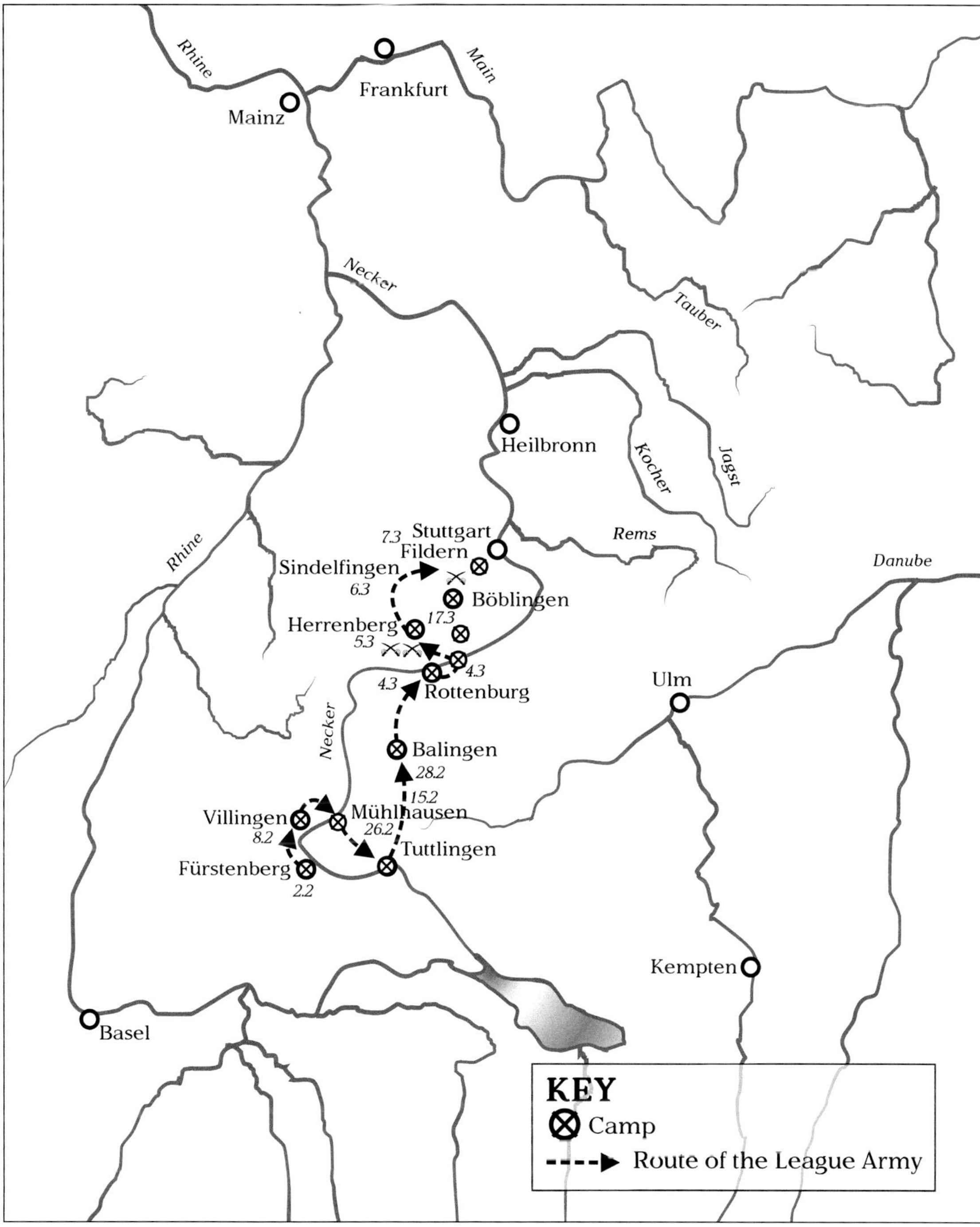

Map 3. The League's campaign route against the peasants of the Hegau and Duke Ulrich of Württemberg.

2.1.3. Swiss Mercenary with halberd and whore (1520–21 by Urs Graf, Kunstsammlung Basel). The Swiss *Reisläufer* could be distinguished from the German Landsknecht by the Cross of St George, which would either be slashed or sewn into into the doublet and hose. For the Landsknecht the diagonal cross of St Andrew was preferred.

Ulrich's army. At Herrenberg, some 30 km to the south of Stuttgart, the Truchsess caught up with the Duke. At this point the League army comprised 1,500 mounted men-at-arms and 5,000 infantry.[8] Marshalled into two main columns, the infantry were protected by five squadrons of horse in the van with two in the rear. They were accompanied by falconets – mobile light artillery pulled by one or two horses which were able to keep up with the columns. The infantry units had sleeves of handgunners positioned in the wings. The Truchsess was forced to retreat following the opening salvos from the Duke's artillery, and once Ulrich had taken Herrenberg a number of other towns – namely Sindelfingen, Böblingen and Leonberg – also fell to him. Stuttgart still remained the Duke's goal, however.

By this time the League members of Bavaria, Franconia, and the Imperial cities had mustered in Ulm, Tübingen, Münsingen and Reutlingen and these companies finally arrived in the Truchsess's camp on 4 March. The supreme commander was determined to prevent Ulrich from fulfilling his objective. He amassed his troops at Esslingen 17 km south-east of Stuttgart. The city council had already sought refuge in Tübingen and requested military aid from the League, unable to place its trust in its own militia. Those recruited mercenaries who made up their protection detail were regarded as nothing more than a 'rabble',[9] who badly needed to be equipped with League weapons and armour. By this time – early March – Landsknechts were making their way back to German soil but it would take some time before sufficient numbers could be recruited.

On 7 March – seen by some as a turning point – the League wrote to its members that Duke Ulrich had made a pact with the peasants and that they were joining him in droves, and that nothing but total mobilisation of the League's full complement i.e. the third 'third' would be required. The total League complement thus numbered 1,892 horse and 10,984 foot. In monetary terms this amounted to a monthly wage and supply bill of 67,844 florins. The League members were asked not to furnish these additional men but to make financial provision for the final third. Driving out the Duke would require the recruitment of foreign mercenaries since one could ill depend on infantrymen drawn from the cities and the farmsteads of Swabia who would either be unruly or, worse still, treacherous. The peasant threat had been the tipping point for the League. The appeal was specifically aimed at the princes in the League (Austria, Mainz, the Palatinate, Hesse, Würzburg, Eichstätt, Bamberg, Constance, Bavaria, Brandenburg, and Württemberg) who were

8 Stadlinger, op. cit., p. 218.

9 Blickle, p. 118.

all asked to consider how to combat the new challenge to the existing order which had emerged from the peasant parliament which was meeting in Memmingen (see section 2.2., The Campaign against the Peasants).

For the Truchsess, preventing Ulrich from retaking Stuttgart was the key. Defeat here for the League could lead to a domino effect throughout the region. It should be possible to defend Stuttgart with a good garrison, particularly since the Duke had left his heaviest artillery pieces at Balingen. A prolonged siege would weaken the Duke since he would run out of money to pay for his Swiss mercenaries. The city councillors in Tübingen agreed, and immediately sent a despatch to their citizens assuring them that they would be protected. Meanwhile the Truchsess ordered a squadron of horse to ride south to prevent the Duke from positioning his cannon within range of the city walls. Ulrich had the logistical problem of transporting 10 culverins and three cannon (*Kartaunen*), the latter capable of firing shot weighing between 40–100 lb. If bridges and roads could be rendered impassable, time could be won to make the necessary siege preparations within the city.

On 7 March the Truchsess oversaw the strengthening of the Stuttgart garrison by some 1,600 foot soldiers and 600 mounted men-at-arms under the command of Ludwig von Helfenstein. Von Helfenstein immediately moved to secure the allegiance of the citizenry and prepared for a siege. On 9 March Ulrich broke camp at Böblingen and marched on the city, and at 3:00 p.m. in the afternoon he began bombarding the suburbs. The Nuremberg and Augsburg companies of the League attempted a sortie but were pinned back by the Swiss *Reisläufer* in Ulrich's ranks. The Duke then attempted to create a breach, rolling a barrel of burning pitch towards the city gates, but the alert defenders were able to extinguish the threat. From records it is clear that there were pockets of League troops positioned in the suburbs, for 40 League mercenaries in the pay of Nuremberg were overpowered by some of the Stuttgart citizenry and forced to absolve themselves from serving the Truchsess for a month.[10]

On the third day of the siege, Ulrich was beginning to get desperate and wrote to his subjects in his territory to rally behind him. The situation was fluid. The Truchsess was highly dependent on an expensive system of messengers to keep him informed of the general mood in the countryside, and critically of the League reinforcements which he could expect. He assured von Helfenstein that reinforcements were on the way in the form of 3,000 infantry which he had recruited and the promise of a further 2,500 men under Wolf Gremlich. The latter, however, was having severe difficulties in finding men, for good numbers of those Landsknechts returning from Pavia were now joining their 'brothers' in the peasant bands.

Ulrich's failure to take Stuttgart appears to have been the last straw for the Swiss in his ranks. They departed on 12 March escorted by a squadron of League horse. A certain Onophrius Setzstab had arrived from Zurich with an instruction to their captains and ensigns to withdraw en bloc in an orderly fashion or face withdrawal of their citizenship. They were, however, tasked

10 Ulrich Artzt quoted in Blickle, p. 124.

2.1.4. The practice of *Brandschatzung* – extorting money from villages and towns to avoid being razed – not only terrorised the peasants but provided a clear and steady source of income for the League's war chest. The process was usually overseen by a designated fire officer known as the *Brandmeister*. The League was at pains to prohibit plunder but if the war chest was empty after a battle and the infantry were due an extra month's pay following a victory, then the probability of ill-discipline if not mutiny in the ranks would be high. On numerous occasions the League's mercenaries cut loose in an effort to supplement their pay where they could. This not only wreaked havoc in the outlying countryside, but disrupted the work of the fire officer whose task it often was to fill the League coffers to meet its own mounting debts. (Woodcut: Erhard Schön)

with bringing Ulrich to safety. The Archduke tried to encourage their desertion by making it known that he would cover their remaining pay and pay a bounty for handing over the Duke. This ploy failed and Ulrich made it safely back to Hohentwiel.

The Truchsess was intent on seeking revenge. Those towns which had pledged allegiance to Ulrich (Herrenberg, Balingen, Waiblingen, Sindelfingen, Rosenfeld and Leonberg) were occupied and taxed up to 5,000 florins to avoid being razed. Some 2,000 went to the League mercenaries and commanders as compensation in place of booty. In Herrenberg, the men were stripped of their weapons, the town gates shortened by four metres and the walls breached in two places. That Ulrich had escaped arrest was a source of great displeasure for the League and questions were asked, particularly by William of Bavaria, regarding the competence of the supreme commander.

2.2. The Campaign Against the Peasants

While the Truchsess was pursuing Duke Ulrich, much of southwestern Germany was in open revolt.[11]

There had been peasant unrest before, notably the Bundschuh[12] uprisings of 1502 and 1513, the Poor Conrad movement of 1514 and a further Bundschuh insurgency in 1517. These had been quite localised. 1525 was a different matter as isolated insurrections began to spread, with peasants and artisans organising into bands (*Haufen*) stretching from the Black Forest, along the Rhine river, to Lake Constance, into the Swabian highlands, along the upper Danube river, and into Bavaria and the Tyrol. This popular uprising was becoming more a 'revolution of the common man' than a simple peasant revolt.[13] Those bands with Landsknechts in their ranks began to adopt a similar military organisation to the League army, although at the outset access to comparable military equipment left much to be desired. On March 7, the same day that the League council was deciding on a full mobilisation

11 Ulrich Artzt, as quoted in Blickle, p. 124.

12 Bundschuh – literally a tied shoe and typical leather footwear of the peasant at the time which was fastened with straps. Contrasting with the thigh boots of the nobility, it came to symbolise class difference and appeared on peasant flags in this early period of resistance, together with the crucifix. Cf. Thomas Adam, *Joß Fritz – das verborgene Feuer der Revolution. Bundschuhbewegung und Bauernkrieg am Oberrhein im frühen 16. Jahrhundert* (Verlag Regionalkultur, Ubstadt-Weiher 2002).

13 Peter Blickle, *From the Communal Reformation to the Revolution of the Common Man* (Leiden: Brill,1998).

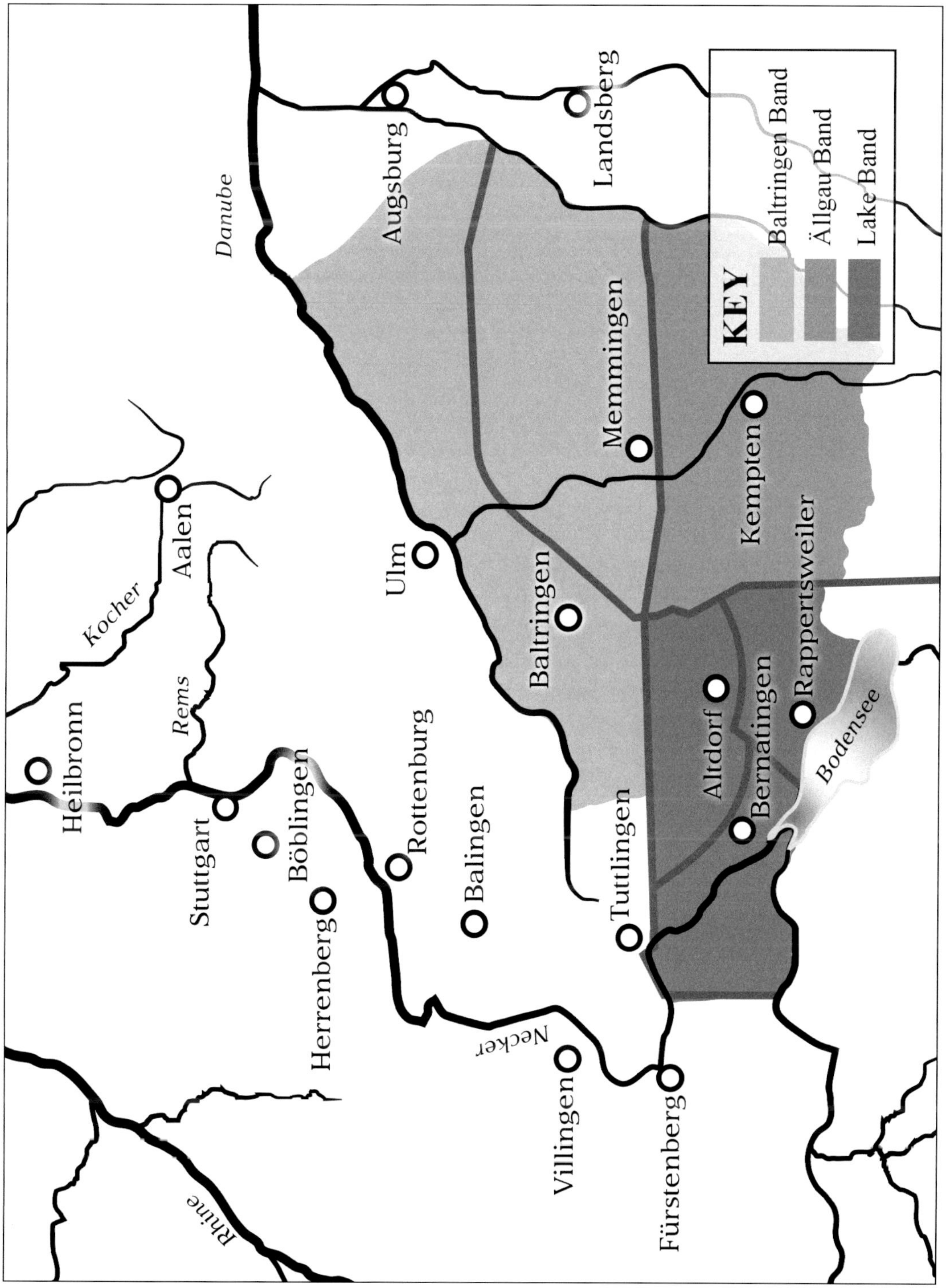

Map 4. The peasant bands of Upper Swabia. This map shows the approximate distribution of the three main peasant armies of Upper Swabia: the Hegau, the Lake and the Baltringen bands.

2.2.1. Cover of the Twelve Articles Pamphlet. Between February 27 and March 1 1525, representatives of the Upper Swabian Peasant bands from Baltringen and the Allgäu and Lake Constance regions met in Memmingen to agree a common cause against the Swabian League. They proclaimed the establishment of the Christian Union, an Upper Swabian Peasants Confederation. This is the title page of that document – the so-called Twelve Articles. Intended as a summary of the more than three hundred articles composed by the Baltringen peasants for presentation to the Swabian League these were published and distributed widely within a matter of weeks. The cover gives an impression of peasant weaponry in the conflict. (Artist unknown)

of its contingents, some 50 representatives of the three embryonic peasant armies of Upper Swabia – the Lake (Constance), Baltringen and Allgäu bands – convened the first peasant parliament at Memmingen and proclaimed the establishment of a Christian Union (*Christliche Vereinigung*). The peasants met again on 15 and 20 March and adopted the so-called Twelve Articles and the Federal Order (*Bundesordnung*).

The Twelve Articles sought to address the main grievances of what was the lowest stratum of society and the one with the highest tax burden at this time. The majority of peasants were tenant farmers who in turn employed agricultural labourers, but the nobility could invoke their rights to forced labour (*Frondienst*) at any time. They were also powerless to prevent their crops being destroyed by their lord's pursuit of wild game and the hunt. Moreover, in the early sixteenth century, no peasant could themselves hunt, fish, or chop wood freely, as they previously had, because the lords had recently taken control of common lands. Should a peasant wish to marry, he required not only his lord's permission, but had to pay a tax. There was also a death tax payable to the lord – usually in kind. There was little redress against feudal injustice since the courts were operated by the clergy or wealthy burgher and patrician jurists. The social order was kept in place by the most horrific forms of physical punishment, backed up by an increasingly corrupt clergy who used the sale of indulgences – in Catholic theology a remission from temporal punishment inflicted by the Church for a previously forgiven sin – to raise vast amounts of money.

The Twelve Articles thus demanded the utilisation of the great and small tithes for public purposes, the abolition of serfdom, death taxes, and the exclusion from fishing and hunting rights; the restoration of the forests, pastures, and restrictions on forced labour, taxes and rents. Finally, they included a demand to end arbitrary justice and administration. The tenor of the meeting and the ensuing pamphlet was very much a religious one: the aim being to 'introduce, encourage, and administer a Christian constitution'. The inclusion of the right to elect and deselect clergymen in the Twelve Articles was thus an important principle. Divine justice had become the battle cry of the peasants in what has been seen as a war of 'biblicism against feudalism'.[14] The Holy Roman Empire was embroiled at this time in the Reformation, a challenge to the Roman Catholic church which had been heralded by Luther's nailing of the 95 Theses against the sale of indulgences on the door of the All Saints church in Wittenberg in 1517. The Prince-Bishops who

14 H.J. Cohn, 1979, 'Anticlericalism in the German peasants' war 1525', in *Past & Present* 83(1):3–31.

were active in the League represented the Catholic church, a faith to which many but not all of the nobility still subscribed. The twin threat which the peasants posed to both the political and religious order had to be suppressed by the authorities. Within two months some 25,000 copies of the Twelve Articles had been printed and were circulating in the Episcopal territories of Bamberg, Würzburg, the Franconian districts generally, Bavaria, Tyrol, and the Arch-episcopal territories of Salzburg. Peasant activity spread north as far as Thuringia, south into the Alpine territories, and west into Alsace and Lorraine. The core of the Holy Roman Empire was astir.

Following the retreat of Duke Ulrich to his fortress at Hohentwiel, the Truchsess remained encamped with the bulk of the League Army at Dagersheim some 25 km south-west of Stuttgart. Elements within the League Council were still advocating a negotiated settlement with the peasants, who had submitted their grievances in writing to the officials at Ulm. The appointment of the Truchsess to supreme commander of the League army had been decided back in February, largely because of the immediate threat posed by Duke Ulrich, which had also been the pretext for the decision to fully mobilise on 7 March. For the hawks within the League, however, the hidden agenda was to use the might of the authorities to smash the peasant insurrection.[15] These orders were duly transmitted to the Truchsess. There was just one problem: could the League rely on its mercenaries to undertake this task?

2.2.2. Landsknechts debating in the 'ring'. (Woodcut from Leonard Fronsberger, 'Fünff Bücher von Kriegß Regiment vnd Ordnung', 1555. Courtesy: Bayerische Staatsbibliothek)

15 Blickle, p. 129.

Following the end of any military engagement there would invariably be tensions within a mercenary army. The Landsknechts were expecting their wages (if not even a victory bonus) and according to Hans Lutz, the Truchsess's herald, had taken control of the artillery park until it was forthcoming. The respective company ensigns left their units as a gesture of their displeasure at the action their men had taken.[16] The stalemate was broken by the eighth day when the men demanded a convening of the *Gemein*, a form of representative organisation which followed a tradition established by the Swiss. Each squad or *Rotte* elected their own representative or *Gemeinweibel* to speak on their behalf at the convening of the so-called *Ring* – a circle in which grievances could be aired, recalcitrants tried, and matters of discipline and day-to-day logistics discussed. On this particular occasion the *Ring* was attended initially by the captains and the squad representatives, who sought to appease the rank and file with the promise of a short sharp campaign against the peasants with the promise of good booty. However, the reaction was not what was expected. When news was reported back to the men, the entire Memmingen contingent including their captain immediately broke camp to return home. Of the Augsburg company, only the captain and seven men remained. Some 1,000 men had de facto mutinied. 'Nobody wanted to take on the peasants', wrote Lutz in his diary,[17] a sentiment echoed by Leonard von Eck who estimated that half of the army was thus disposed, particularly those recruited from the Lake Constance region.[18] There were at least three reasons for a refusal of the League's infantry to march against the peasants. Firstly, they were their countrymen and, in many cases, literally their own flesh and blood. Secondly, in times of stand-down (known as the *Gartzeit*) it would be the peasants they would turn to for employment or handouts. Thirdly, as Ambrosius Geyer observed, many in the League's rank and file had been caught up by the new Reformist thinking.[19]

The Truchsess was faced with a potential catastrophe. His standing within the League hierarchy was already placed in jeopardy by his failure to apprehend Duke Ulrich. If his army now fell apart, so too would his reputation and the established social order along with it. He immediately despatched his commander of the infantry to persuade them to return to camp. Wilhelm von Fürstenberg succeeded in convincing a good number to turn back. Having convened a *Ring*, the Truchsess then rode in so that he could address an assembly of the representatives of his rank and file. At first the supreme commander appealed to the piety of his men. He argued that the peasants had not risen in the name of God – they had resorted to violence, in itself a violation of the Gospel. Some of his commanders had become victims of their rampages in their absence and they had even resorted to plundering priories and churches. This apparently only had limited effect on those assembled, for only 15 hands were raised in acknowledgement of

16 Baumann, 1998, p. 40.

17 Quoted in Blickle, p. 133.

18 Wilhelm Vogt, *Die bayrische Politik im Bauernkrieg* (Nördlingen:Becksche Buuchhandlung, 1882), p. 409, quoted in Blickle, p. 133.

19 Quoted in Baumann, 1998, p. 41.

this point with the majority of these belonging to officers. His second line of argument then focused on their means of livelihood, namely that they depended on the nobility for their pay. If they abandoned their companies now they would never again be allowed on any muster lists in the land. Moreover, if the peasants were to prevail they would then become their servants. Finally, he ended by arguing that if they failed to side with him, they were free to go and never return, whereupon he rode out the *Ring* leaving the officers and rank-and-file representatives to return to their companies to brief their fellow mercenaries and decide whether to remain in the League army. Michael Fressman, captain of the Augsburg *Fähnlein* which had been persuaded to return to camp, succeeding in convincing his men to stay, but the Memmingen, Constance and Black Forest contingents could not be swayed, and left. The Truchsess wisely chose not to discipline these men although technically this was mutiny which was punishable by death. Given the numbers of men – estimates vary between 1,200 and 4,000[20] – executions on this scale would have not only exacerbated an already tense situation but could also have caused a major conflagration within the ranks.

2.2.3. Heralds were originally messengers sent by monarchs or noblemen to convey messages or proclamations. Like other officers of arms, a herald would often wear a surcoat, called a tabard, decorated with the coat of arms of his master, in this case the colours of Swabia. Hans Lutz was herald in the League army and as such was constantly at the side of the Truchsess and despatched on numerous occasions to open negotiations with the enemy. It is not known whether the herald depicted here is Lutz as a more likely motif would have been the three lions of the House of Waldburg. (Sammelbandmehrerer Wappenbücher – BSB Cod.icon. 391, [S.l.] Süddeutschland (Augsburg?), um 1530 [BSB-HssCod.icon. 391]. Courtesy: Bayerische Staatsbibliothek)

Those who elected to remain sent two delegates – Hans Lutz himself, and the captain of the Brandenburg–Ansbach company to reassure the Truchsess that he could depend on these men who were ready to take the fight to the peasants. Their resolve may have been strengthened by rumours that a number of Landsknechts had been brutally murdered by peasants at Kristenfegen, and the Truchsess himself had received news that 'new blood' was on its way in the form of the thousands of Landsknechts who were returning from Northern Italy.[21] These would be men who were battle hardened and seeking to avoid the prospect of immediate unemployment.

The mutiny at Dagersheim was a wake-up call for the Truchsess, who set about re-establishing order and discipline within his army. New rules of engagement were drawn up, particularly to deal with the problem of booty. There was an unwritten rule that following a victory the soldiers could boost their pay with what they were able to plunder.[22] However this could lead to conflict within the ranks, devastate the countryside, and crucially deprive the League of a possible source of income particularly needed to cover the rising cost of keeping such an army in the field. It was necessary to regulate this practice, and the Truchsess collected proposals from his officers which

20 Baumann, p. 189; Bensing and Hoyer, p. 74.

21 Baumann, p. 42.

22 Baumann, p. 90.

led to the introduction of the practice of 'fire extortion' rather than plunder. In essence a tax would be imposed on the households of a defeated territory against the threat of property being razed to the ground. He appointed two fire masters (*Brandmeister*) who oversaw the appointment of a further two such officers for the rank and file and horse respectively. The aim was to set a tariff by which two-thirds of whatever was raised by this means would flow into the League coffers while the remaining third would be paid out to the men as an additional bonus. According to estimates from von Waldburg's scribe, by the end of hostilities the League ought to have appropriated 900,000 florins in fire tax with some 300,000 being distributed amongst the soldiers – a monthly bonus of 30 florins on top of the official 20 as laid down in their contracts (the campaign lasted five months).[23]

We can assume that at some time late in March there would have been a new muster at which those men who had committed to marching with the Truchsess against the peasants were sworn in. Here a new set of articles of war would have been read out to the men which reasserted the authority of the supreme commander, fixed the command structure and reminded them of the severe consequences of desertion. His mercenaries would only be entitled to an additional month's pay following a victorious battle if the men had acted on the orders of the supreme commander. The League army had by now received orders to march to Ulm, where there was considerable peasant activity in the surrounding countryside. Efforts on behalf of the peasants to bring about change were at this point still political as they attempted to submit the Twelve Articles for acceptance by the authorities. Negotiations were therefore still underway as the League army approached Ulm with an apparent truce agreed until 2 April.[24] Elements in the League, however, were still searching for a pretext to declare war. This was soon to be found.

On 27 March the castles at Laupheim and Schemmerberg were attacked by peasants from the Baltringen band, having been provoked by the murder of one of their delegates.[25] On the same day there were skirmishes between Landsknechts of the League and groups of peasants between Ulm and Ehingen. This was sufficient for both parties to declare a breach of the truce. Although the Baltringen band of peasants was a major cause for concern, the League headquarters felt harder pressed by events in and around the towns of Leipheim and Günzburg and ordered the Truchsess to march on Leipheim to the east of Ulm, from where news had arrived that a peasant army was mobilising.

Leipheim

At the beginning of the sixteenth century Leipheim was a small market town where local farmers sold their grain and flax. The craftspeople in the town, primarily handweavers, were legally and economically dependent on the city of Ulm. However, the weavers of Ulm had succeeded in largely dominating the local market by reducing the number of handlooms which had resulted

23 Quoted in Blickle, p. 140.
24 Blickle, p. 147.
25 *Ibid.*, p. 146.

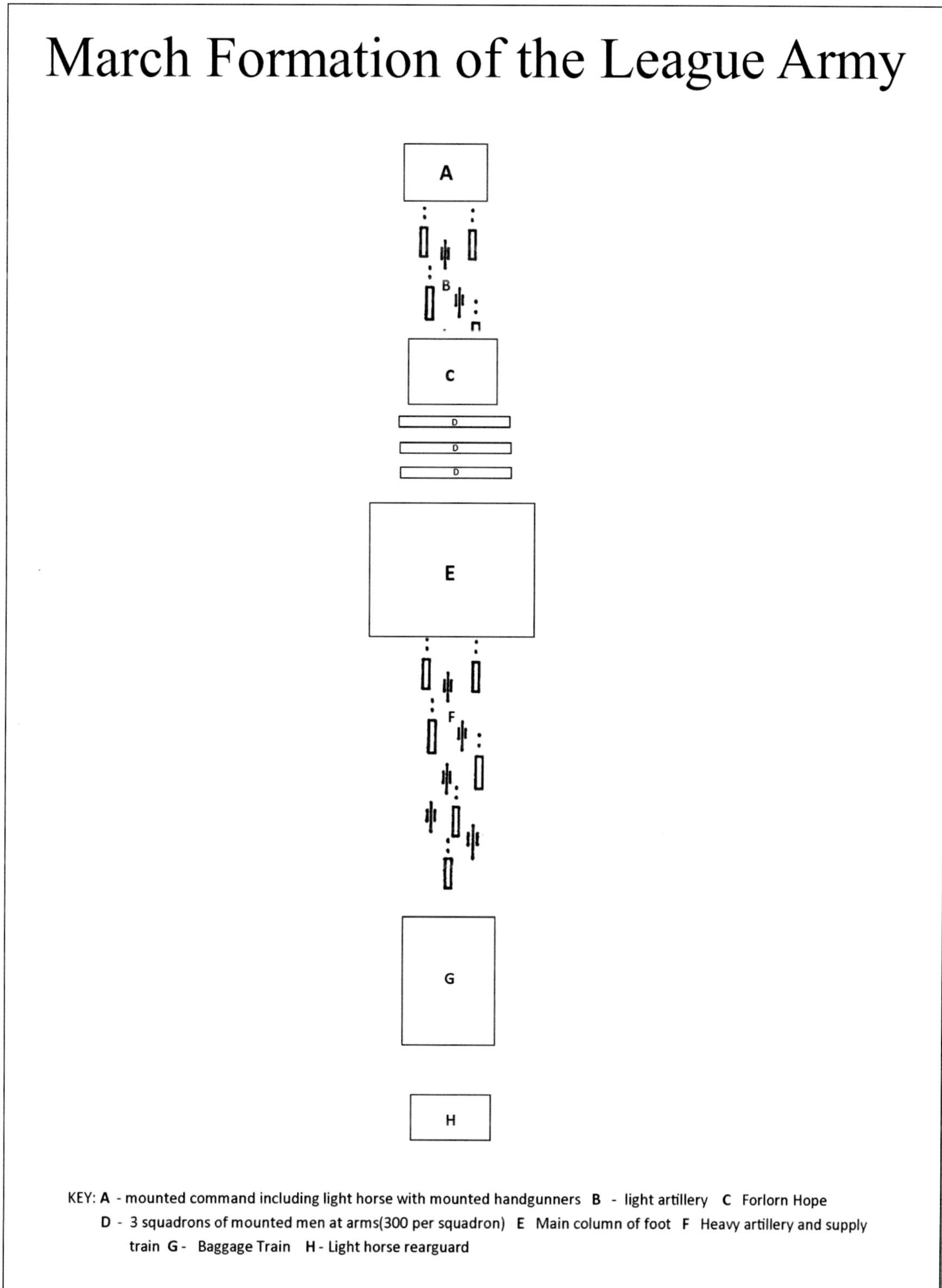

2.2.4. A diagrammatic representation of an army on the march, based on a description of The Truchsess's scribe of the League army departing from Ulm for Leipheim. Contemporary depictions of armies on the march reveal units of infantry and horse and artillery strewn out across the countryside, however.

in job losses in Leipheim. Successive petitions to the authorities in the city had generated little response. The town became a focal point of unrest in the region involving the villages of Illerthausen, Krumbach, Yettingen and Nau.[26] On 18 February groups of peasants began to organise at Weissenhorn. The Leipheim band, which formed itself into a military unit, drew on men from over 100 villages in the area. At the beginning of March envoys were sent to Ulm to negotiate with the Swabian League. When it became apparent that few concessions would be forthcoming, the peasants began to mobilise in earnest. The Leipheim band under the command of a local pastor by the name of Jakob Wehe numbered some 5,000–6,000 men.[27] Contemporary accounts relate a degree of surprise on the part of the authorities at the extent to which the insurgents were armed,[28] despite basic weaponry being available consisting of a dagger, hammer, axe or club. These additional weapons and armour had been acquired either through the sale of plunder from the churches or from arms and armour taken from nearby castles. The band had also succeeded in plundering four artillery pieces from the castle at Bühl. Wehe had built up a war chest and a substantial supply train of 60 wagons. His immediate objective was the town of Weissenhorn where the wealthier guildsmen and the patriciate supported the Swabian League. A garrison of 340 horsemen had been hastily despatched to the town by the Count Palatine and the gates remained firmly closed to the peasants, with only bread and wine being passed over the wall. On hearing of the approach of the League army and fearful of exposure to the League horse on open terrain, Wehe ordered his men to retreat to Leipheim where conditions would be more favourable.

As early as 29 March a reconnaissance of Leipheim was ordered and a spy despatched into the town. The scout was, however, discovered and in the ensuing melee a peasant was shot dead and another taken prisoner. The spy escaped and reported back that the Leipheimer band could be defeated with no more than 400 horse.[29] On 1 April the Truchsess received his orders to bombard Leipheim. Ordnance would be made available in Ulm. En route he was to raze villages to the ground or extort monies from the same to help fund the campaign, and recruit any Landsknechts returning from Italy to the League cause. On 3 April his vanguard reached Ehingen while the main column of foot was leaving the outskirts of Ulm.

The Leipheim band were conscious of the impending battle and despatched a messenger to the Ries peasants with a request that they send 2,000 men as reinforcements while at the same time penning a conciliatory letter to one of the League commanders, Wilhelm von Fürstenberg, calling

26 Erich Broy, *Reformation und Bauernkrieg*, in Erich Broy, Heinz Bühler, Rudolf Mögele, Siegfried Ortlieb, Werner Schmidt, Georg Simnacher, Josef Weizenegger (eds), *Leipheim. Heimatbuch einer schwäbischen Stadt an der Donau* (Weissenhorn: Konrad, 1991), 61–120, 83f.

27 Hoyer, p. 152; Adolf Laube, Max Steinmetz und Günter Vogler, *Illustrierte Geschichte der deutschen frühbürgerlichen Revolution* (Berlin: Dietz,1974), pp. 244–246; Franz, 1924, op.cit., p. 17.

28 Günther Franz, *Der deutsche Bauernkrieg* (Berlin: Deutsche Buch-Gemeinschaft, 1926), p. 16.

29 Franz, p. 17.

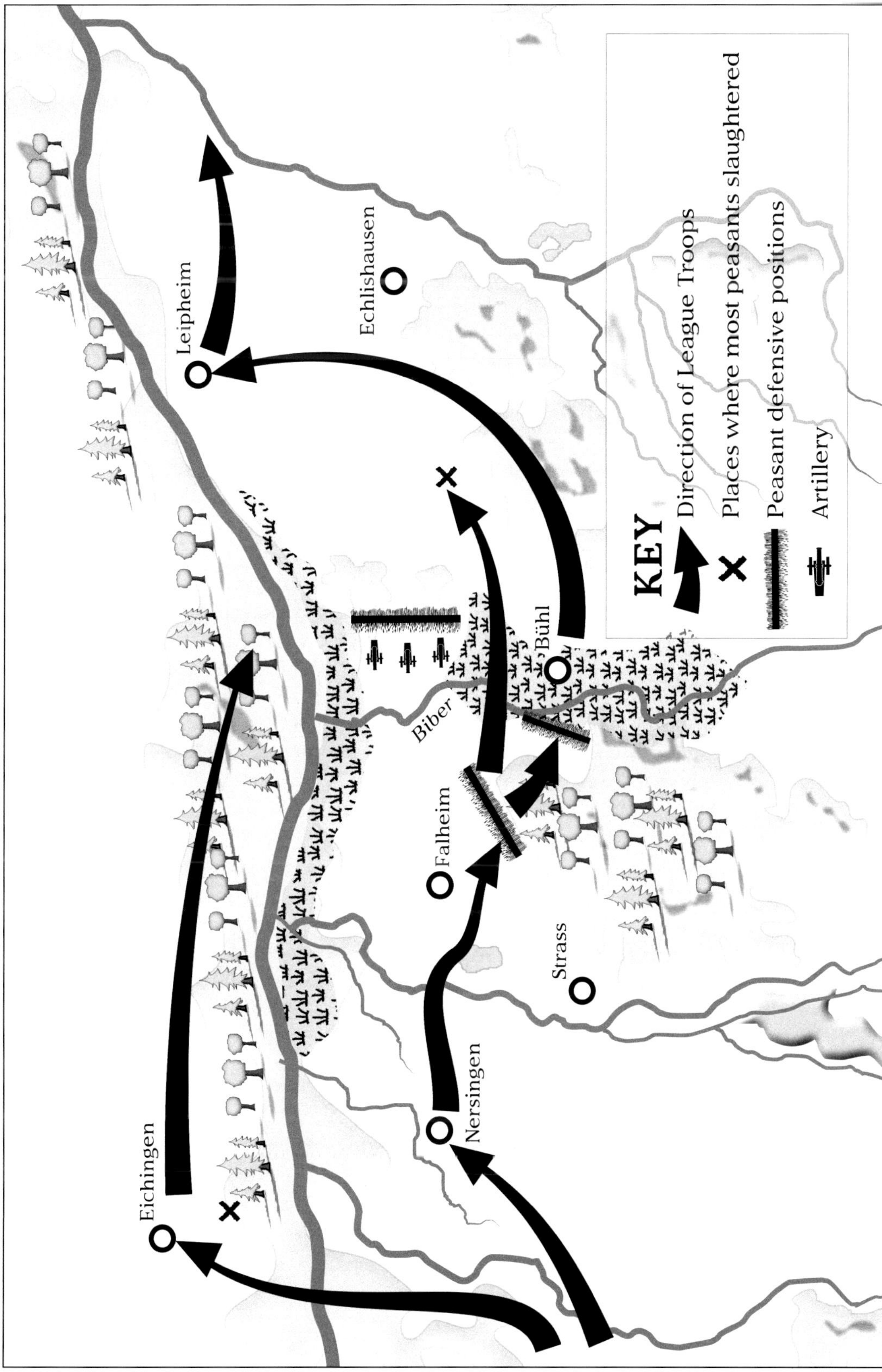

Map 5. The Battle of Leipheim, 4 April 1525.

for a peaceful resolution of the state of affairs. On the morning of 4 April, the main column of the League broke camp before the gates of Ulm and began their march on Leipheim.

The Truchsess took the decision to divide the mounted men-at-arms in the van into two units. One troop of Ulm and Hessian horse was despatched under the command of Sigmund von Berg to keep to the north bank of the Danube to drive out those peasants engaged in plunder at the priory at Elchingen. They were to proceed towards Leipheim where they would meet up with the rest of the army. Meanwhile Waldburg would lead the second troop along the south bank of the river, approaching Leipheim via the village of Nersingen to the west of the town. This troop consisted of companies of Bamberg and Würzburg horse, and a forlorn hope from Mainz accompanied by five falconets.

The latter units were confronted by two strategically placed peasant defences at the crossing where the Biber tributary meets the Danube. According to Geyer, the peasants had assumed a battle formation behind this wagonfort. The Truchsess ordered his falconets to open fire prior to giving orders for the League to advance.[30] However, the marshy terrain prevented him from committing his light horse to a frontal assault. He ordered his light horse to make a flanking manoeuvre through the village of Bühl to cut off any peasant retreat to Leipheim. The manoeuvre was successful. Lacking the necessary military discipline, the peasants broke ranks and beat a retreat to the town through a small wood. Some were successful, others made for the Danube marshes where the League horse would not be able to reach them. In the ensuing panic they met two companies of peasant reinforcements from Günzburg who had difficulty in getting their fellow rebels to turn and make a stand. They too were cut down by the advancing League horse followed by the Mainz forlorn hope. As many fled across the floodplain they were either caught by the League horse or escaped into the Danube where those who could not swim perished.[31] Those who were able to swim across the river were met by von Berg's men. A slaughter ensued. Von Berg's Ulm and Hessian horse were also met by some 2,000 peasants from Langenau who had plundered the priory at Elchingen a day earlier. These were swiftly routed and either put to the sword or also chased into the Danube where many perished. The actual number of casualties is unclear. Christoph Fuchs reported some 3,000 peasant casualties and 1,000 taken prisoner.[32]

According to Georg von Waldburg's scribe, the supreme commander was not yet content with his victory and deployed his infantry who had by now arrived with the main artillery train just outside the town, where he felt there was still a large number of rebels. Fearful of a damaging bombardment, the town councillors despatched an elderly citizen and a number of older women beyond the town walls to plead for mercy with the Truchsess. It was agreed that Leipheim would have to give up its radical cleric Jakob Wehe and compensate his men, in return for leniency. Having taken Leipheim,

30 Ambrosius Geyer, quoted in Blickle, p. 160.

31 Vocheser quoted in Blickle, *ibid.*

32 Quoted in Blickle, p. 160.

the Truchsess now had to contend with his mercenaries who were desperate for plunder. Worried that matters could get out of hand, particularly that a number of his Landsknechts would desert once they had looted sufficiently, he summoned Wilhelm von Fürstenberg to join him in addressing his infantry.

Fürstenberg had somewhat prematurely promised his infantry that the town of Leipheim would pay each man a month's wages (four florins) as a mark of their victory. The League horse was offered the same terms for those townspeople of Günzburg, whom they had forced to surrender. The people of both towns spent the night under armed guard in their respective churches. Desperate to avoid rampaging mercenaries, the Leipheim leaders offered up 150 citizens for ransom. However, in order to meet the promise of twice a monthly wage this would have meant the town having to find 32,000 florins – a completely unrealistic prospect. When the League mercenaries realised this money could in no way be forthcoming, they mutinied. Once again, as at Dagersheim, Georg von Waldburg was faced with a serious situation. A mutiny could only mean two things: the mercenaries rampaging through the town plundering any assets to which the League felt entitled, and then deserting with the potential of substantial sections of his army transferring lock, stock and barrel across to the peasant cause. Only by promising that the League would cover the outstanding amount within a month could the mutiny be averted.

The mutiny caused a postponement of any executions of the ringleaders from the morning of 5 April until midday. The previous day, whilst his men were still engaged in the rout of the peasants, Truchsess had already requested Ulm to send Berthold Aichelin, the official provost. Jakob Wehe, the spiritual leader of the Leipheimer band, was manacled together with Jörg Ebner, Ulrich Schön and Melchior Harolt, and paraded in a circle assembled before the Truchsess for judgement. Denying any wrongdoing and refusing to confess to anyone but God himself, Wehe was beheaded along with the other ringleaders. The pastor of Günzburg was spared for reasons unknown, although his future actions were to be severely restricted.

With the surrender of neighbouring Langenau, the Leipheim uprising had been roundly broken. Now came the task of extracting reparations. The Truchsess ordered his *Brandmeister* to complete a register of peasants living in the outlying villages and hamlets. A list of 4,075 names was compiled covering 114 named places. These individuals were to be the targets for the extortion of money and assets which the League badly needed in order to prosecute its campaign.[33] This amounted to reparations amounting to 1,500 florins plus a 'fire prevention tax' of six florins per household. In addition, the town was stripped of its rights and placed under the yoke of the authorities in Ulm. Some citizens were expelled while orders were given for the town gates to be removed from their hinges and the wall to be breached in two places.[34] Some two months later the League army would pass by Leipheim once more on its way to crush the Allgäu peasants, but the social, economic and political

33 Brey, p. 101.
34 Brey, p. 99.

damage wreaked by the League on the people of Leipheim and its environs would take much longer to dissipate.

The aftermath of Leipheim was assessed in different ways by members of the League. Ulrich Artzt felt that executing the ringleaders, commanders and ensigns was no way to put an end to the peasant uprising and that it would serve only to antagonise their subjects even further. The princes on the other hand had only praise for the Truchsess with Philip of Hesse particularly effusive, offering the League 1,000 horse, providing, of course, they would cover their costs.

Notwithstanding this victory there was still tension between the supreme commander and his political overseers. The Truchsess insisted on a convening of the council of war, for it was the council which determined the ongoing strategy, but also would have to bear responsibility for any failures in decision making. Receiving his new orders, he broke camp on 12 April to march south towards Baltringen, the epicentre of peasant activity in the area.

Baltringen

The village of Baltringen had achieved notoriety in the spring of 1525 since an alleged army of 18,000 peasants had adopted its name for their band. However, as the League army marched south, a peasant army was nowhere to be seen. Leonard von Eck had wanted the League army to engage with the Baltringen, Allgäu and Lake bands in one action but this turned out to be too premature. The Truchsess felt compelled to report that the Baltringen band had to all intents and purposes dispersed. Some peasants had surrendered and were despatched to Ulm to plead for mercy by indicating their readiness to swear an oath of fealty to the League. Some contingents in the band returned to the Truchsess's own territory of Waldburg, others retreated to the forests where they would be difficult to track down.

On its approach, the League's *Rennfahne* encountered a troop of 100 peasants who had sortied from a fortified churchyard, and put them to the sword. The Truchsess entered Baltringen at the head of 400 horse with the intention of extracting protection money from the villagers. The villagers were charged twice on the grounds that they had been involved in attacks on the priories at Ochsenhausen and Heggbach. As the light artillery caught up with the *Rennfahne*, the falconets were deployed to bombard the neighbouring village of Sulmingen. A number of peasants were put to the sword in nearby Mietingen. A day later the League began issuing communiqués from their headquarters in Ulm announcing that the Baltringen band was no more – its commanders having surrendered to the authorities.

2.2.5. Seal of the Baltringen Band (Courtesy: Franz Liesch)

When the League army began to arrive the Imperial city of Biberach, the Truchsess was denied access by the parish council. This served to reinforce the view that the Imperial cities (including both the parish and city councils) were coming down on the side of the peasants. As the army continued south, the League's mercenaries were indiscriminate in their treatment of the peasants regardless of whether they had sworn an oath of allegiance to the League. Even the Abbot Jakob Murer, who was no supporter of the peasant cause, was compelled to observe in his chronicle that the League army had been particularly 'cruel in their punishment of the peasants'.[35] At Ummendorf, a village close to his abbey, the League horse had 'let their dogs loose' on the bakehouses, wells and even a cemetery in their search for peasant plunder. There are records of the shooting of a peasant and the hanging of a rebel who had stolen a chalice from the parish church.

As a knight commander of the League army, the Truchsess still sought honour through victory on the field of battle. There would indeed be honour particularly in routing a peasant army which measured up to the League's own. News began arriving that such an army was assembling near Ravensburg just north of Lake Constance. Going against League orders he turned eastwards following the River Iller. Beyond Ummendorf he encountered two companies of peasants which were swiftly defeated by his light horse, and some 300 taken prisoner. A third company retreated to a nearby wood where some sought refuge up in the trees. The League arquebusiers engaged in target practice as they despatched these rebels from the branches. One hundred

2.2.6. The arrival of the League army at Ummendorf. This shows the banners of the Truchsess of Waldburg, Count von Helfenstein and the League banner. (Illustration from the chronicle of Abbot Jakob Murer from the monastery of Weissenau, © Waldburg-Zeil'sches Gesamtarchiv SchloßZeil, Leutkirch, ZAMs 54)

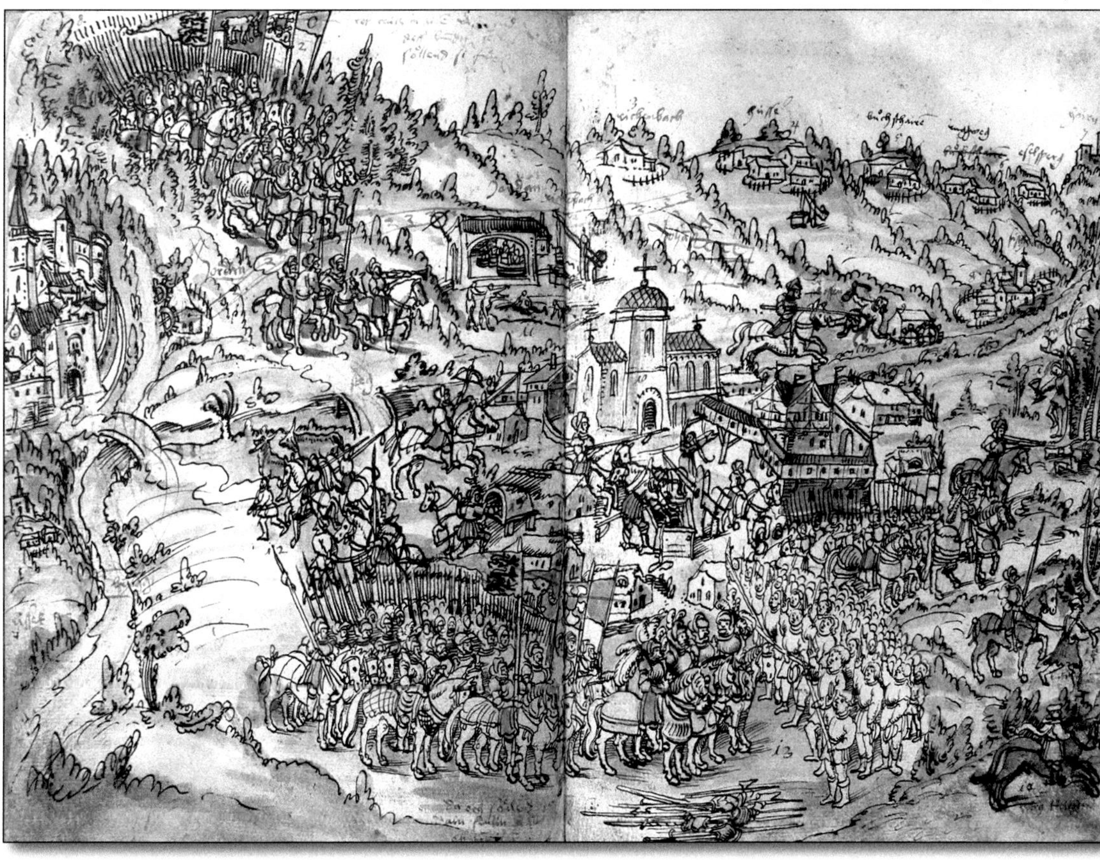

35 Jakob Murer, *Die Weissenauer Chronik* (Stuttgart: Jan Thorbecke Verlag, 1997), p. 33.

and fifty peasants are said to have perished including the captain. Four rebel officers including the ensign were taken prisoner, and it is thought, executed.

Leading the campaign had meant that the Truchsess had not been able to pay attention to his own dominions within the county of Waldburg notably Waldsee, Wolfegg and Zeil. His peasants had set fire to a manor house at Linden, taken some of his own servants prisoner, and set their bail at 4,000 florins. It was impossible for him to enter into direct negotiations with his people so he despatched a letter reminding them of their place as his subjects and demanding that they desist from their actions. In response his peasants called for the establishment of a committee to negotiate their demands. The letter was signed by a Florian Greisel, a pastor who had been appointed by the Truchsess himself and who now was commander of the Lower Allgäu band. This enraged von Waldburg and instead of marching west on Ravensburg he turned east towards Wurzach where the band had assembled.

Wurzach

Some 4,000 peasants had taken position in front of the town near the Wurzach marshes, and around midday negotiations commenced with them. The Truchsess demanded the surrender of Florian Greisel and all the rebels' weapons and armour. These talks dragged on, enabling the League army to take up a better position on a hill by the leper hostel on the road to Ravensburg. Deploying his forlorn hope to the front with his artillery positioned just behind, his main column of foot consisting of his companies from the Elector of the Palatinate, Austria, Mainz, Bamberg and Würzburg took up position to the right of the artillery. To the left waited his light horse (*Rennfahne*) and his companies of arquebusiers,[36] followed by squadrons of horse of Hesse, Bavaria, the Margrave of Brandenburg, Eichstätt and the remaining nobility. When it became clear that Greisel would not be offered up, the Truchsess ordered his trumpeters to sound battle, whereupon his forlorn hope opened their ranks to reveal the artillery which fired three salvos into the peasants. In the ensuing panic some peasants lost their way in the marshes – it was by now nightfall – where they were caught by the League light horse and forlorn hope. Some, according to despatches from von Waldburg's scribe, fled into the town. Accounts vary as to the extent of the slaughter. A more conservative estimate puts the dead and captured at 1,400.[37] For those able to escape, some protection could be found near Weingarten where a sizeable and well-equipped peasant army had assembled. Whilst the general consensus has been that the peasants were ill equipped for this conflict, musters reveal a different picture. The village of Aichstetten in von Waldburg's own domain of Zeil was able to provide 113 men, 12 of whom were armed with pikes, 23 with boar spears, and 22 with halberds. A further nine provided handguns and four were armed with crossbows. Fifteen men wore half body armour, and a further four had breastplates.[38]

36 It is not clear from the accounts whether these companies were mounted or not.

37 Blickle, p. 171.

38 Blickle, p. 174.

It was now time to suppress the Lake band. The League army left Wurzach on 15 April and after a march of some 12 kilometres encountered the peasants at Gaisbeuren, 16 km to the north of Ravensburg. His scouts reported a force of some 7,000 peasants and Landsknechts[39] in a favourable position with a forest to the rear and marshland to the front. Following a day long cannonade from both sides, the peasants withdrew to Weingarten just outside Ravensburg. Pursuing the peasants to Weingarten, the Truchsess was now faced with a substantially bigger peasant army, against which a pre-emptive assault by his mounted men-at-arms would, in his view, have been foolhardy given that his main column and artillery would take some time to catch up with the van. Moreover, news had arrived that peasant reinforcements from the Hegau and Black Forest were on the way.

Potentially a peasant army of some 20,000 men was in the process of assembling, including a substantial number of well-trained soldiers (*Knechte*). As was customary before any military engagement a parley was arranged and four delegates from the Allgäu and Lake Constance bands rode into the League camp to discuss terms. The Truchsess demanded the surrender of the peasant banners and all arms and armour in return for an arrangement tabled by the League three weeks previously whereby three towns were to be appointed by the peasantry and three by their lords, to negotiate and settle all disagreements amicably, legally, and bindingly. Negotiations dragged on for four days. The peasants declined to offer up their weapons: not only were these the (costly) tools of the trade of the thousand Landsknechts in the ranks, they were also needed by the peasants who belonged to the local militias. For the militant members of the ranks this amounted to outright capitulation. Although the Truchsess did not succeed in disarming the peasants he was able to politically neutralise the Upper Swabian rebellion by negotiating the so-called Treaty of Weingarten, which was intended to achieve peace in the region, the tearing up of the peasant banners and return of 'the great cannon, eight pieces in all, to the places whence they had taken them.'[40]

For the Truchsess there were ramifications. Some, indeed almost the majority of the Estates of the League were discontented that he had accepted such a treaty with the Allgäu and Lake Constance band behind their backs. There was an argument that despite being outnumbered he had wasted an opportunity to smash the insurgents. In a letter from the territorial clerk at Ravensburg to the territorial bailiff of Upper Swabia the former wrote:

> I was able to see this at Castle Ravensburg, where several cavalrymen and foot soldiers argued that Truchsess Georg could have put the peasants to flight if he had ridden into the Lake Constance and Allgäu bands with some horsemen on the field at Weingarten as they were bringing up their vanguard from Berg to Weingarten, for both peasant camps were a cannon's shot away from each other, and having taken up their position in considerable disorder and ranged their

39 Numerous mercenaries returning from Pavia had elected to join the Lake band.
40 Extract from a Letter from the territorial clerk at Ravensburg to the territorial bailiff of Upper Swabia 5 May 1525 in Scott & Scribner pp. 157.

2.2.7. The signing of the Treaty of Weingarten. (Detail from the Weissenauer Chronicle of Abbot Jakob Murer. © Waldburg-Zeil'sches Gesamtarchiv SchloßZeil, Leutkirch, ZAMs)

> artillery with great difficulty, they could have been taken by surprise and seized, as many observed.[41]

The hawks in the League were bitterly disappointed, particularly since the treaty could not be wholeheartedly ratified by the peasants. There were still outbreaks of resistance in the Truchsess's own territory.

The events at Weingarten occurred over the Easter festival, and while the Lake and Allgäu peasants were availing themselves of the wine and food stored at the priory of Weissenau,[42] and the League army rested up in their camp at Gaisbeuren, matters were taking a turn for the worse in Weinsberg, Franconia. Here the peasants had a much more militant and irreconcilable view of the nobility. On Easter Sunday Count Ludwig of Helfenstein, who had defended Stuttgart on behalf of the League against Duke Ulrich, had been seized by peasants of the Neckar Valley/Odenwald band who had stormed his castle and captured the countess and her children:

> They then led lord Ludwig, Count of Helfenstein … to a field in the direction of Heilbronn and with him thirteen nobles, among whom were two ensigns, Rudolf von Eltershofen and Pleickhart von Ruchzingen. There they made a circle and made the well-born and the noble run the gauntlet with their servants, twenty-four persons in all. The count offered to give them a barrel of money if they would let him live, but there was no way out but to die. When the count saw that, he

41 *Ibid.*

42 The events were captured vividly in the account written and illustrated by Jakob Murer, the abbot of Weissenau.

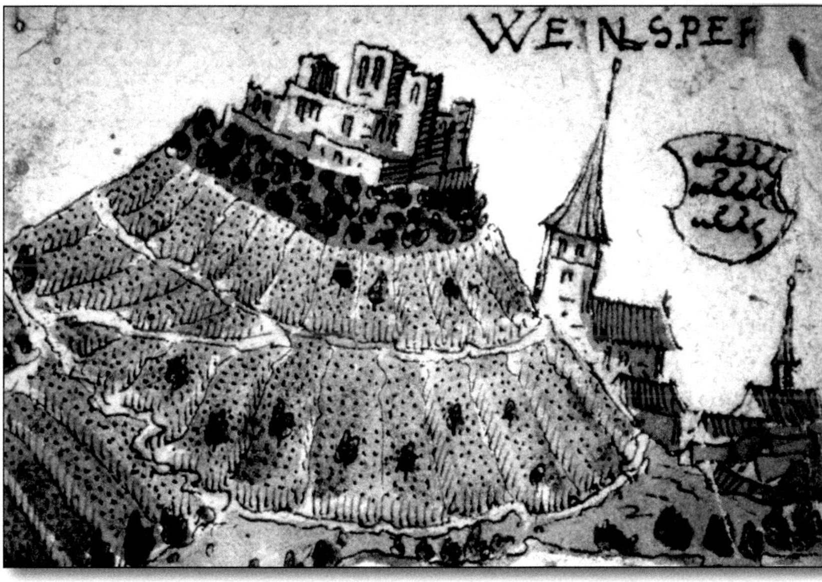

2.2.8. Weinsberg – scene of the turning point in the Peasants' War.

> stood stock still until they stabbed him. Rudolf von Eltershofen went into the ring with his arms crossed and gave himself up willingly to death. Thus, all these were driven through the lances contrary to all the rules of war and afterwards dragged out naked and let lie there. May Almighty God have mercy on them and us! After all this, they set alight to the castle and burnt it, and then marched off to Würzburg.[43]

Weinsberg was to prove to be a turning point in the Peasants' War. As news spread so too did outrage on the part of the nobility. Von Helfenstein would have to be avenged. Moreover, the repeated calls from League members in Franconia for assistance against the rebels would now have to be heeded.

However, two major issues concerned the Truchsess and would have to be dealt with before he could march north: the growing suspicion of his military leadership on the part some members of the League, and more seriously the continued presence of substantial pockets of unrest in Upper Swabia, with the Hegau and Black Forest bands particularly active, and the Württemberg peasants now posing a threat. Since the outset of the campaign, Georg von Waldburg had repeatedly requested of the League that they send officials so that he might convene councils of war to provide the necessary legitimacy for his chosen course of action. Given the perceived unsatisfactory outcome of Weingarten, the League organised a delegation of representatives of the three estates under armed escort to meet up with their supreme commander. It took them a week to reach the camp in Weingarten.

The council took the decision, despite ongoing activity from the Hegau peasants, to march north to crush the Württemberg insurgents. The Truchsess did his utmost to delay the march but was overruled by the council, much to his annoyance. Finally, on 28 April the army broke camp and began their

43 'The Massacre of Weinsberg 16 April 1525'. Report of Parson Johann Herolt. Translation in Scott and Scribner, p. 158.

march towards Herrenberg and Böblingen, both in the direction of Stuttgart. To their rear the Hegau peasants continued their unrest. In early May an edict issued by Charles V pronounced the bloody events at Weinsberg as an act against the Holy Roman Empire. This galvanised the princes in Mainz, Trier and the Palatinate, as well as the Margraves of Hesse and Baden into action. But Weinsberg had a similar effect on the peasants. Two peasant bands under the command of Matern Feuerbacher and Hans Wunderer had mobilised in Württemberg, prompting the officials in Stuttgart to seek refuge in Tübingen, from where they pleaded with the Truchsess to come to their assistance. The combined bands were camped at Herrenberg some 30 km south of Stuttgart and 20 km from Tübingen, and had issued their own programme for constitutional reform. Unlike other municipalities in the territory which had opened their gates to the peasant army during their march, Herrenberg refused them access. The town had been severely punished for collaborating with Duke Ulrich and wished no further trouble from the authorities. Moreover, the League had garrisoned a company of Landsknechts there. Herrenberg was for many peasants a symbol of Habsburg rule.

Both peasant commanders were determined to rout the approaching League army and despatched riders to enlist the help of the Allgäu, Black Forest, Hegau and the remnants of the Lake bands. The Black Forest band heeded their call and arrived at Herrenberg, whereupon the town was placed under siege on 8 May. The siege lasted all day until early evening when the peasants succeeded in blowing up the town gates, undermining the walls and setting a number of houses within the walls alight with flaming projectiles. The League garrison was taken and imprisoned and their money confiscated.

On hearing the news, the Truchsess immediately ordered his horse to advance on the town. The following day 1,600 horse deployed for four hours in front of the gates without any movement. The peasant bands had set up two squares on the slopes of the Manor house at Herrenberg with a third unit behind a wagon fort in front of the town. The Truchsess ordered up his heavy cannon to a hill opposite the manor house and a company of arquebusiers, who exchanged fire with the peasants in the wagon fort. Both sides were no more than a mile apart but did not engage. That night the Truchsess ordered the outlying villages to be razed and the livestock in one village was taken and ransomed back to the peasants. Under pressure they petitioned the Truchsess for protection for the women and children against his rampaging Landsknechts.[44]

Expecting to launch a full-scale assault the following morning, the League mercenaries awoke to find that the peasants had vacated the town and marched 15 km north-east to Böblingen and Sindelfingen leaving a handful of wagons and carts behind in their camp. Herrenberg could swiftly be retaken and the imprisoned garrison freed to join the League army, which was now ordered to hastily continue its march in pursuit of the peasants. A half a mile from Böblingen and Sindelfingen they halted and set up camp for two days. On 12 May orders were given for an assault, and as the League army

44 Quoted in Blickle, p. 201.

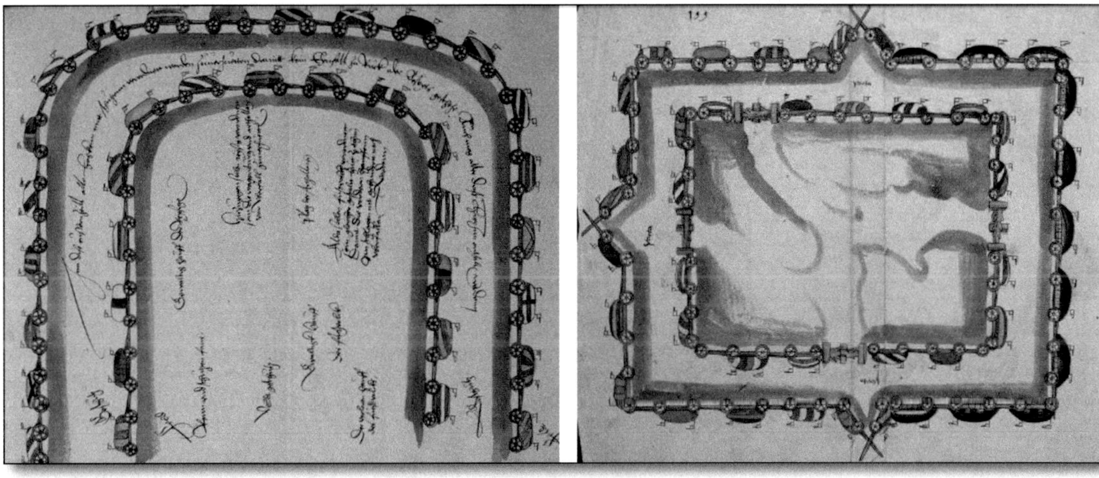

2.2.9. League army encampments en route would have been drawn up behind the supply wagons for protection. Military commentators at the time offered different wagon fort layouts. These two are illustrated in Franz Helm's 1535 *Buch von den probierten Künsten* (Cod. Pal. germ. 128. P. 195v. Courtesy: Heidelberg University Library)

approached the peasant bands formed three squares in front of a wood near Sindelfingen. The Truchsess deployed his mounted arquebusiers to force the peasants out of their advantageous position but they were beaten back by a unit of peasant horse and their own handgunners. While this skirmish took place the League army was able to enter Böblingen and the Truchsess ordered the deployment of 300 arquebusiers and two wagons with hook guns[45] to fire upon the peasant squares. The main League column meanwhile set up on the hill behind the town and commenced an artillery barrage on the peasant positions. The peasants returned fire and a two-hour-long cannonade did little to alter the course of the battle. The peasants were the first to mount an infantry assault – the intention being to retake Böblingen.

However their forlorn hope was soon pinned back by a hail of shot from the League handgunners positioned on the walls of the town. The League light horse then followed through, aided by the arquebusiers who pointed out where the peasant troops were positioned. In the ensuing melee 300 peasants were killed and eight falconets taken. Joined by a further four squadrons of light horse and a unit of mounted handgunners, the League pursued the retreating forlorn hope which crashed into the main rebel column, causing panic to ensue and insurgents to scatter in all directions.

2.2.10. Böblingen, by Andreas Kieser. How the town would have looked at the time of the battle.

45 Hook guns were characterised by a protrusion from beneath the barrel, enabling the gun to either be mounted on a wooden bipod or positioned between the crenellations of a town or castle walls.

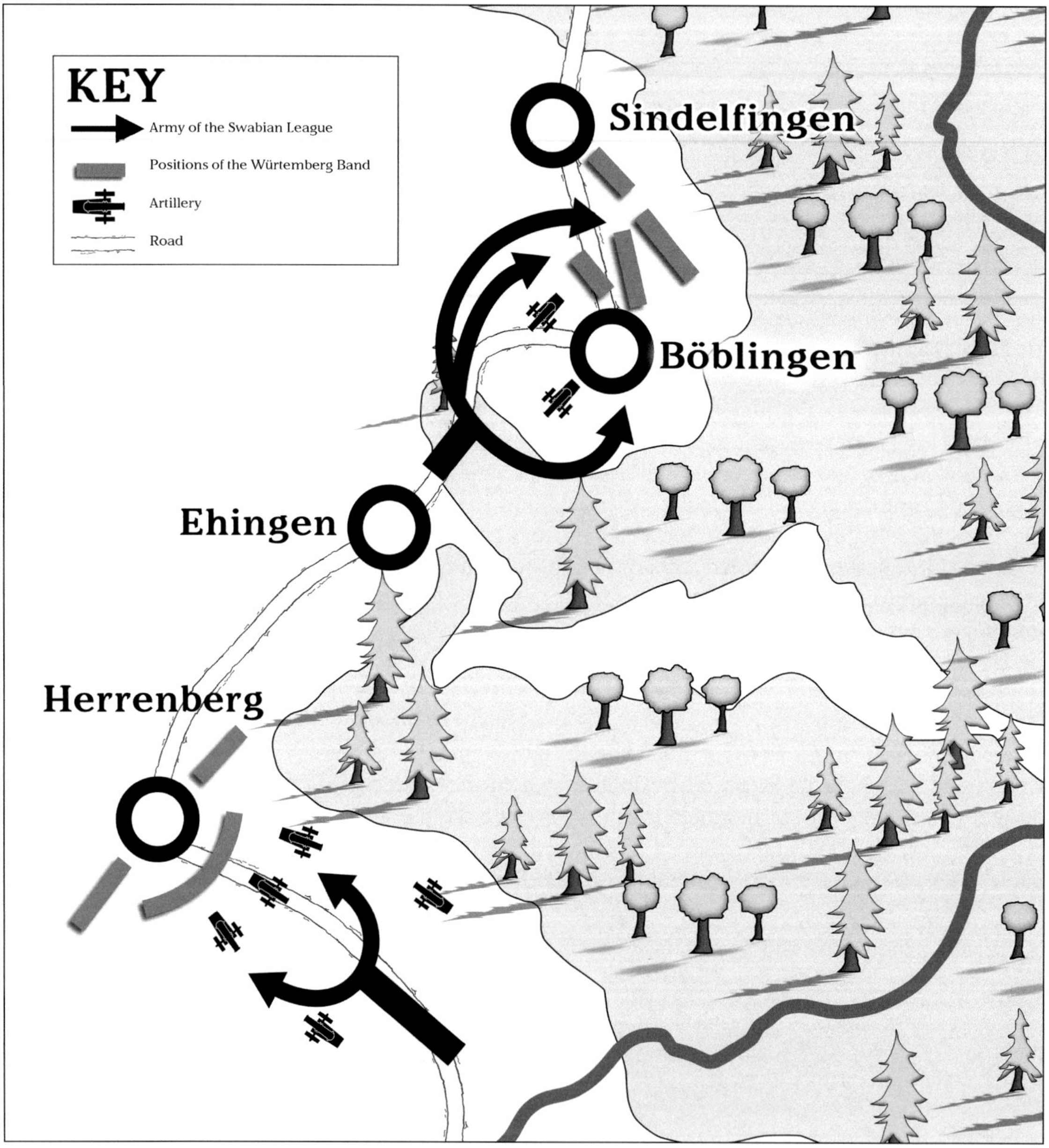

Map 6. The Battle of Herrenberg-Böblingen, 12 May 1525.

The battle had lasted four hours. Twenty-two pieces of artillery and baggage wagons were taken,[46] along with 12 peasant banners.[47] Figures vary between 5,000 and 8,000 for the numbers of peasants slain against only 50 League casualties. The Truchsess was keen to press on with the two-day march north to Weinsberg, but as his army was about to break camp, news arrived of the capture of one of the arch-perpetrators of the murder of Count von Helfenstein – Melchior Nonnenmacher. Nonnenmacher was a piper who had performed for both the Count and the Truchsess on occasions. On hearing that he had donned the Count's hat and danced and played while von Helfenstein ran the gauntlet, the supreme commander ordered that he be roasted to death in a symbolic act of vengeance.

The way was now clear for the march on Weinsberg, where it was believed that the combined peasant bands of Swabia, Franconia and the Neckar valley had assembled. However, on arrival at Weinsberg there was no peasant army to be seen. Having spent some five weeks encamped in and around the town and castle they had marched east in the direction of Würzburg. On their march to the town the League army scouts captured one of the leaders, Jäcklin Rohrbach, who met the same fate as Nonnenmacher. The Truchsess was in no mood for appeasement and on arrival promptly ordered the removal of all livestock and food supplies from the buildings, which were then set alight. Once again, however, the army command had to contend with unrest within the rank and file who were frustrated by the ban on plunder imposed by the League. The Landsknechts refused to move any further with the army whiling away on the outskirts of Weinsberg. The Truchsess had to pay out 15,000 florins before they could continue their march in pursuit of the Franconian peasants.

The Defeat of the Franconian Bands

The uprising in Franconia had developed relatively late with three large bands forming between the beginning and the middle of April. The Tauber valley band, with its epicentre in the town of Rothenburg, drew on disaffected elements from countryside and towns within the diocese of Würzburg and Mergentheim. They had adopted the Twelve Articles of the Upper Swabian peasants but made explicit the demand for the appropriation of all castles and the establishment of equality before the law. The Neckar Valley/Odenwald band had its origins in the Archdiocese of Mainz – specifically around Oberschupf in the Odenwald. This had been significant in past efforts to mobilise resistance to the authorities, particularly in the earlier Bundschuh movements. The third army, known as the Bildhausen band, formed on 12 April taking its name from a Cistercian monastery near the town of Munnerstadt in Lower Franconia, where some 300 peasants had gathered to address the heavy taxes and forced labour imposed by the monastery.

The monastery was set alight and the abbot and his monks were forced to flee. The activities of these three bands had resulted in a particularly grave situation for the nobility and clergy since they had effectively lost political

46 One estimate put it at 33 (Blickle, p. 202).

47 *Ibid.*

control in the region. Wherever the bands marched the nobility and clergy had been forced to adopt their programme and swear an oath of allegiance. The scribe of Georg von Waldburg lists some 20 nobles, towns and priories which had 'crossed over' to the peasant cause including some of the Truchsess's personal enemies.[48] The leadership of the Franconian rebels, including the knight Götz von Berlichingen, the nobleman Wendel Hipfler and an official of the archdiocese of Mainz Friedrich Weigandt, had called for a political convention of all the peasant bands of southern Germany with a date set for mid May in Heilbronn, which functioned to all intents and purposes as the rebels' capital in the region. The assembly never happened. By mid May the League army stood before the gates of Heilbronn, as the League Council had ordered the Truchsess to come to the aid of the three most threatened members: the Bishop of Würzburg, the Margrave of Brandenburg and the Electors of the Palatinate.

Meanwhile in Würzburg, the regional capital, there was chaos. Prince-bishop Konrad II von Thüngen had fled to Heidelberg, having handed over command of the fortress Marienberg to his bailiff, Sebastian von Rotenhan on 5 May. On 8 May the combined Franconian bands set up camp in Heidingsfeld some five kilometres due south of the city. Their council, including sections of the Würzburg citizenry, opened negotiations with the authorities in Würzburg demanding the transfer of the Marienberg fortress into their control. Following prolonged talks, a decision was taken to lay siege on the stronghold. On 14 May the peasant artillery began to open fire. On the 15th the first assault took place on the outer defences but the peasants were repulsed with the loss of 400 men. After numerous failed attempts to storm, and reinforcements of heavier artillery,[49] the modest garrison in the Marienberg still held firm. On the 23rd the Neckar Valley/Odenwald band withdrew. The siege had failed.

Following the razing of Weinsberg, the League army marched westwards into Kraichgau. In Bruchsal, the Truchsess handed over the peasant leader Pastor Anton Eisenhut to the Elector Ludwig of the Palatinate, where he was beheaded along with two other ringleaders. Following efforts to extract reparations from the rebellious Kraichgau peasants through *Brandschatzung*, the Elector's army joined forces with the Truchsess and marched northwards to the Tauber valley, reaching Neckarsulm on 26 May. Together the army now numbered some 3,200 horse and 9,000 foot. The Bishops of Würzburg, Trier and Strasbourg together with Ludwig and Prince Ottheinrich were now in the overall command group. Against them stood a combined peasant army in excess of 20,000 men,[50] but the rebels still felt it was necessary to reach out to Duke Ulrich of Württemberg for assistance. There was no response. Moreover, Götz von Berlichingen, a knight commander of the peasants with considerable military experience,

48 Blickle, p. 231.

49 Rainer Leng, 'Bauern vor den Mauern – Technische und taktische Aspekte des Sturms auf die Festung Marienberg in Würzburg', in Franz Fuchs, Ulrich Wagner (eds), *Bauernkrieg in Franken* (Würzburg: Königshausen u. Neumann, 2016), pp. 141–80.

50 Blickle, p. 235.

2.2.11. Fortress of Marienberg, Würzburg. (Photo: Christian Horvat)

chose at this crucial moment to relieve himself of his command and return to his residence at Hornberg. He had already displayed less than trustworthy allegiance to the peasant cause in his efforts to prevent the storming of the Marienberg. Large sections of the peasant army were now withdrawing from Würzburg in the direction of the Tauber valley. As the League army marched northwards from Heilbronn it encountered two companies of peasants ensconced in Neckarsulm. After a three-hour artillery bombardment they surrendered. After Weinsberg the Truchsess was in no mood for mercy. Those insurgents who were taken prisoner – here some 40 captains, ensigns and reformist clerics – were executed.

Some two days march north east of Neckarsulm, lies the town of Königshofen in the Tauber valley. Numbers of the Neckar valley/Odenwald band had drifted back to their home villages, but the remainder, perhaps 2,000 strong, retreated there, at the junction of Umpfer brook and the Tauber river. Reinforcements from villages and towns in the region had been arriving in the meantime. It has been argued that the rebel leaders were that day not expecting to face the entire League army there.[51] When the League *Rennfahne* was spotted around midday in the Umpfer Valley, there seems to have been some consternation but no panic in the rebel camp. The Tauber ford at Königshofen was defended with artillery while the main rebel force

51 Michael Bletzer, *Prospectus of Archaeological Research on the Peasants' War Battlefield Of Königshofen, Main-Tauber-Kreis, Badenwürttemberg, Germany* (Texas: Department of Anthropology, Southern Methodist University, Dallas, 2010).

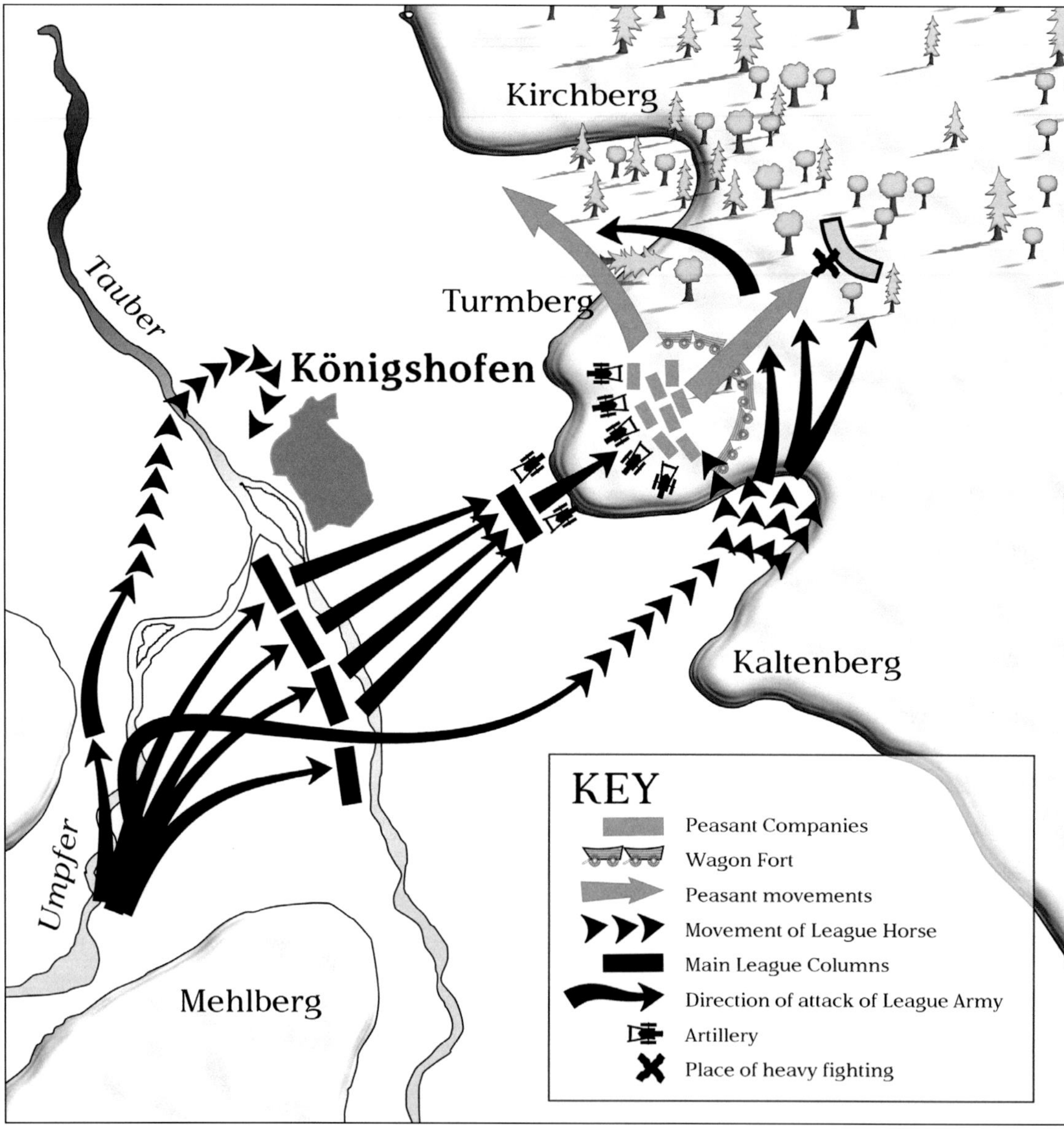

Map 7. The Battle of Königshofen, 2 June, 1525.

relocated to the top of the Turmberg, a hill to the east of the town. According to several sources, this included the movement of some 300 wagons and up to 40 artillery pieces. Given the quantity of heavy equipment and the difficulty of ascending the steep flanks of the Turmberg, it seems likely that some sort of camp had already been set up, probably near the old *Wartturm* or watch tower which afforded a commanding view of the Umpfer Valley. It was around this watch tower that the rebels set up a wagon fort. In this location and with their artillery intact, they might be safe from cavalry attack.

The Truchsess summoned his council of war to determine tactics, and there was little consensus.[52] The majority in the command group argued for the army to take the hill opposite the peasants' position, but Georg von Waldburg felt that this would have little impact on the peasants and would allow them to beat an easy retreat. He succeeded in convincing his commanders to do precisely the opposite: Frowen von Hutten and Ulrich Marschall were assigned 300 horse each and tasked with outflanking the peasants on each side. This, however, would require crossing the ford in the valley, exposing them to peasant artillery fire. Having survived this, they were able to then swerve out of range of the peasant guns and take up positions on the same level as the peasant army. They were followed by two 1,000 strong units of Hessian and Palatine foot. Meanwhile in the valley below, the main column prepared itself for a forward assault on the peasant position once there had been an artillery barrage. The Truchsess himself accompanied the *Rennfahne* to reconnoitre the strength of the peasants and ordered his units to move closer to their position. At some point the peasant command including Georg Metzler cut through the traces of the carthorses, mounted them and made off.[53] In contemporary accounts this has been reported as an act of cowardice but alternative interpretations describe this as an attempt to fetch reinforcements.[54] Given the approaching main frontal assault by the League *Gewalthaufen*, many peasants began to make a run for it across open ground to a wooded outcrop near Deubach.

2.2.12. Landsknecht Pikemen. Handling the pike required considerable training. It is generally considered that pikemen tended to come from the uplands whereas the use of the halberd was drilled in the municipalities. Pikes were between 3.8 and 4.5 metres in length and later versions bore langets which reinforced the point at the head of the staff. A pike cost approximately a florin. (Woodcut: Erhard Schön)

52 Blickle, p. 237.

53 Lorenz Fries, *Die Geschichte des Bauernkriegs in Ostfranken.* Teil 1, 313–4 quoted in Blickle, p. 239.

54 Jürgen Wolfarth, *Die Bauernkriegsschlacht auf dem Turmberg von Königshofen 2. Juni 1525: Die Quellen sprechen eine andere Sprache* (2010), available at <http://www.traumaland.de/html/2__juni_1525.html> (accessed 24 September 2018).

As they dispersed, the League light horse was able to cut them down at will. However, a block of rebels some 1,000 strong was able to resist the cavalry attack and reach the wood where they quickly erected some basic natural defences against the horses from branches and shrub. There now followed a lengthy attempt by the League foot to oust the peasants, who it is reported were armed with matchlocks: '… the footsoldiers who came up later could not get at them, although armed with long pikes, and they resisted until nightfall.'[55]

The rebel resistance must have been considerable, for according to his scribe, the Truchsess himself suffered a wound to his knee with a polearm. Finally, they were broken: '… then these peasants begged that their lives be spared, which was promised them by the soldiers. And so these peasants were led off down to the parish church of Königshofen, where they were held prisoner and ransomed; those who could pay the ransom were released …'

By nightfall several thousand lay dead. It is estimated that there were between 6,000–8,000 casualties.[56] Wilhelm von Fürstenberg was placed in charge of the prisoners. Those who were not successfully ransomed were carted off in the baggage train to Heidingsfeld. There were mixed emotions amongst the League command: some cheered against the sound of drums and trumpets, others openly wept. The army returned to the foot of the hill where they camped. The command group spent the night in the town.

The following morning saw once again a repeat of an all too common occurrence in the League campaign. As reported by Lorenz Fries, the secretary to Konrad Thüngen, Prince-Bishop of Würzburg:

> The league's footsoldiers had it written in their contracts that when they had won a battle or storming, they would be paid their wages. Now since the peasants had been defeated. they wanted to have their battle pay, which saw the end of their month's service and the beginning of a new period of pay. But the princes, captains, and military councillors were opposed to this, saying that the battle was won entirely by the horse and that they, the foot, had not arrived. So, they were not obliged to pay them anything. But the league's soldiers stood their ground, and the next day, when camp was struck to march to Würzburg, they refused to march and remained at Königshofen.[57]

Von Waldburg's initial response was to continue his march on Würzburg with his horse, his captains and his *Doppelsöldner*.

The situation was in a state of flux. Some 10,000 peasants and citizens of Würzburg had mobilised and were marching in the direction of Königshofen when they learned of the peasant defeat. On learning this from his scouts, the Truchsess decided to engage despite having a weakened army which was bereft of the bulk of his infantry. As they came to Sulzdorf, they faced a large band of peasants ensconced behind a wagonfort. As the League horse

55 Blickle, op. cit.

56 *Ibid.*

57 Report of Lorenz Fries, *Die Geschichte des Bauernkriegs in Ostfranken*, Teil 1, 313–4 from Scott and Scribner, p. 294.

attacked, the peasants broke ranks and were pursued across the open ground. Lorenz Fries estimates that some 5,000 were slain, and reported that the roads towards Ochsenfurt up to a quarter of a mile from the town were strewn with dead peasants.[58] As they reached Ingolstadt near Giebelstadt many peasants fled into the woods. Several hundred sought refuge in a village chapel which was then set alight by the League horse.[59]

A further group probably numbering around 250 ensconced itself in the ruins of the castle belonging to the family of Florian Geyer (himself a rebel leader). Initially the rebels had thrown their hats into the air as a sign that they wished to surrender but when no signs of mercy were shown they barricaded themselves in further, holding off the League troops for some three hours:

> They had carried up a great pile of stones to barricade the gate [but the League] brought up guns into position in two places … and bombarded it – Although the peasants defended themselves so manfully that they were able to repel the league's first attack. they soon tired and became exhausted from the effort of carrying stones in the castle, digging earthworks, throwing [missiles] and defending themselves.
>
> The league was greatly vexed that those in the castle could hold them at bay for so long, and became so heated with shame and anger that they redoubled their efforts. They stormed the castle afresh and conquered it, killing whomever they found inside. That went on throughout the night. Some peasants had hidden themselves in a cellar, but the league's soldiers threw straw into it, strewed powder over it, and set it alight. However, it is reliably reported that three of them survived, and when the league marched away, they climbed out during the night and escaped.[60]

The League reported a major victory. Ambrosius Geyer put the number slain at 6,000[61] – others present were more modest in their estimates. Significantly, in these two battles, large swathes of townspeople had perished alongside the peasantry. Eighteen heavy pieces of artillery, a number of heavy arquebuses and several wagons were captured. The victory was sufficient to prompt those striking Landsknechts who had remained in Königshofen to rejoin the ranks of the League army.

Following Ingolstadt, the League took over the camp at Heidingsfeld, some five kilometres south of Würzburg, which had served as the Franconian rebels' base. The Truchsess once again needed to resolve his differences with his men. The despatch riders from Ulm arrived with orders to impose hefty fines on the citizens of Würzburg and Bamberg for their involvement in the uprising. Fire masters had been appointed and they were to carry out their

58 *Ibid.*

59 Sebastian Schertlin von Burtenbach, *Leben und Thaten des weiland wohledlen und gestrengen Herrn Sebastian Schertlin von Burtenbach : durch ihn selbst deutsch beschrieben ; nach der eigenen Handschrift des Ritters urkundlichtreu* (Münster: Aschendorff'schen Buchhandlung, 1858), p. 5.

60 Fries, *ibid.*

61 Ambrosius Geyer, in F.L. Baumann, p. 742.

work. This placed the supreme commander in a quandary. There was unrest amongst his infantry which needed to be quelled. If fines were to be levied then this should not mean that his men were forbidden from plundering livestock and moveable goods too. The Truchsess found himself in a position where he was supporting action contrary to the rules of engagement and his own principles in order to keep the peace within his army. The League officials responded that following the taking of Würzburg, the army was to be engaged for a further two months. The outstanding debts owed by the League members were to be settled. The League had liabilities of some 200,000 florins – a huge sum.

Given these overarching financial constraints, the only way in which the army could continue was by relaxing the ban on plunder which was to be strictly organised through each squad or *Rotte* of 10 men. Any artillery plundered had to be handed over to the League as well as prisoners, since they would either be ransomed or – as in the case of ringleaders, ensigns and officers – tried and executed. Despite this the Truchsess felt obliged to come to an immediate agreement with his men on their pay. They were to receive a backdated 'battle bonus' (*Schlachtensold*) of four florins – an amount which he personally vouched for – in return for their unbridled support for the rest of the campaign.[62]

Now Würzburg needed to be retaken. On 5 June the Truchsess demanded that the city surrender to the League. Some 5,000 peasants were still within its confines. Waldburg ordered units of horse to patrol the outskirts; nobody was to be let in or out. On 7 June the city finally capitulated and a city delegation rode into the camp at Heidingsfeld in a desperate attempt to plea for mercy. The Truchsess's terms were severe. Each house was to pay protection money of 10 florins to the League, all leaders would be punished but the remaining peasants would be allowed to return home against a pass. All weapons and armour were to be handed over and the citizens were ordered to swear a renewed oath of allegiance to the Bishop, who was to determine the amount of reparations to be levied on the citizenry. All former rights and privileges would be restored provided the townspeople were to sever all ties with any organised peasantry.[63]

No quarter was given to the ringleaders. Following a triumphal entrance into the city, three places of assembly were chosen at which the Truchsess in full armour paraded ringleaders, banner bearers and commanders, who were beheaded before the citizenry. Their heads were placed between their legs and left displayed for days to leave people in no doubt about the consequences of challenging the authority of the Bishop and wider nobility. Peter Haarer, the scribe of Ludwig the Elector Palatine, reported some 76 souls who met their fate at the hands of four executioners.[64] The final act was the demilitarisation of the city. Over 100 wagons were loaded with arquebuses, halberds, pikes,

62 Quoted in Blickle, p. 245.

63 Ulrich Wagner, 'Die Stadt Würzburg im Bauernkrieg', in F. Fuchs and U. Wagner, *Der Bauernkrieg in Franken* (Würzburg: Königshausen u. Neumann, 2016), pp. 113–140.

64 Peter Haarer, *Wahrhafte und gründiche Beschreibung des Bauernkriegs* (Halle: Max Niemeyer, 1881), p. 90.

2.2.13. Following Weinsberg in particular, the Truchsess was merciless in wiping out any further resistance. This coloured woodcut depicts summary executions of peasants in the Franconian uprisings. Some were more staged, particularly where towns were involved. Note the quite plain garb of the mounted men-at-arms. (Photo: Gerhard Raab, Bamberger Burgenbuch. Courtesy: Staatsbibliothek Bamberg)

partisans, swords, daggers, and armour and driven across a ford near the monastery at Himmelspforten, and all cannon, powder and shot including those borrowed from Rothenburg were taken up to the castle, rendering Würzburg a defenceless city.[65]

The routing of the Franconian rebels marked a second major strategic triumph for the League army but there were still pockets of resistance which required attention in Rothenburg, Schweinfurt and Bamberg. In Bamberg, where the uprising had been predominantly anticlerical in nature, some 400 citizens had hurriedly left the city for Nuremberg on hearing of the approach of the League army. Accounts tell of villages either side of the route from Würzburg to Bamberg being ransacked and set on fire.[66] The remaining citizenry were ordered to gather in the square in front of the cathedral, where 12 ringleaders were beheaded and those present were required to swear an oath of allegiance to the Bishop. The rash actions of the Truchsess had prompted a Nuremberg member of the war council to demand a proper trial for those leaders who had been apprehended.[67] Indeed the council of war was becoming alarmed at the way in which the army seemed to be out of control as it trundled through the Bamberg archdiocese.

With Franconia to all intents and purposes under control it was time to take stock. The mood amongst the rank and file, as reported back by the captains, was that if the men were to paid what was owing them, good numbers would depart for their homelands. They had profited from the plunder during this campaign. Moreover, the men were in no mood for any forays into

65 Wagner, op. cit.

66 Blickle, p. 251.

67 *Ibid.*, p. 252.

2.2.14. Pass mark of the Swabian League which served as a pass which was hung out on the walls of property (farms and priories) as a protection from arson or plunder by the League army. (City archive Augsburg Reichstadt Literaliensammlung Nachtrag 111)

the Black Forest or the Hegau. Even the mounted troops seemed to be ill-disposed to continue.[68] By now an enormous baggage train had built up too. The council of war debated whether to dissolve the army at this point and recruit afresh under new command.[69] Names considered were Georg von Frundsberg, Mark Sittich von Hohenems, Burkhard von Hohenems, der Lange Kaspar and Jakob von Wernau. However, the harsh reality was that 7,000 fresh fighting men would be difficult to recruit and most of the possible commanders who came into the frame were otherwise commissioned.

The League army left Bamberg on 22 June. The Truchsess had been ordered to return the heavy artillery to Ulm and take the infantry and light artillery near to the priory at Elchingen. This would take the League army back to where their campaign against the peasants started – near Leipheim. But it meant passing the city of Nuremberg – a member of the League which had been become increasingly unhappy about the actions of the army en route. Formal complaints were lodged by the city to the League council concerning the waylaying by League troops of traders using the routes between Bamberg and Nuremberg. As a League member, the city was nevertheless obliged to provide safe passage to the army but as news reached its citizens of the devastation caused by the Truchsess's men, there was consternation. Whole streets and alleys were barricaded to prevent access, lest there be more wilful plunder, and in the Nuremberg hinterland, Swabian League pennants –pass marks –were hurriedly nailed up on properties to prevent their ransacking.

2.2.15. In one of the pamphlets published in 1525 describing the events of that year, could be read: 'Houses are burned; fields and vineyards lie fallow; clothes and household goods are robbed or burned; cattle and sheep are taken away; the same as to horses and trappings. The prince, the gentleman, or the nobleman will have his rent and due. Eternal God, whither shall the widows and poor children go forth to seek it?' Quoted in E.B. Bax, *The Peasants' War in Germany*, 1899, p. 386. (Woodcut: Hans Behaim)

68 Letter from von Eck to Duke William, June 20, quoted in Blickle, p. 254.

69 Correspondence of Ulrich Artzt, quoted in Blickle, p. 254.

Bamberg had been the northernmost point which the League army had been entitled to reach. Beyond, it had no jurisdiction. Here, in Thuringia to the north, the combined armies of Philip of Hesse, George of Saxony and Duke Henry of Brunswick had smashed the peasants at the battle of Frankenhausen a month earlier.[70]

Despite the League victories in Upper Swabia, Württemberg and Franconia, there were still substantial pockets of peasant resistance in the Allgäu and the Hegau, the Habsburg lands of the Tyrol, and the mining territories in Schwaz, Austria. With a somewhat weakened army the Truchsess now needed to return to his own territory to finally put an end to the peasant scourge. The Hegau rebels had been dealt with by an army raised by Archduke Ferdinand under the command of Mark Sittich von Ems and Count Felix von Werdenberg, in early July.[71] In the Allgäu, however, the revolt continued.

Following the signing of the Treaty of Weingarten the representatives of the Allgäu band had felt betrayed and made it known that they were not bound by its terms. As a member of the Christian Union, the band had begun to arm immediately following the Battle of Leipheim. Between the 4th and 8th of April a number of castles had been stormed with Liebenthann, Wagegg, Sulzberg and Rettenberg, in particular providing a valuable source of weapons, artillery and powder. What wealth had been plundered was used to hire Landsknechts, and efforts had been made to hire additional artillery from the city of Memmingen. However, the city had turned down their request. In the intervening period the band had established close links with other disaffected peasant groupings so that by the end of June in excess of 10,000 peasants had assembled at Leubas in the Allgäu.

On 9 June the League had sent 200 mounted men-at-arms and 700 Landsknechts to deal with developments in the Imperial city of Memmingen, which had demonstrated a clear anti-Catholic tendency in line with the preachings of Ulrich Zwingli, the leader of the Reformation in Switzerland. A number of ringleaders, notably Sebastian Lotzer (scribe of the Baltringer band) and Christoph Schappeler had escaped the League's attentions along with 40 other citizens. Of those who had remained, five were executed and the city was ordered to ransack those properties connected to the peasant cause and to expel any family members. On 12 June the peasants had returned and encircled the city. Peasant numbers had swollen to an estimated 20,000, encamped in two villages on the outskirts of the city.

On 17 June the Truchsess was given the orders to raise the siege of Memmingen. He undertook a forced march having replenished his army to a certain degree with new recruits. The new complement stood at 6,000 foot and 1,500 horse. Records show that the League needed to re-equip the

70 D. Miller, *Frankenhausen 1525* (Seaton Burn: Blagdon Publishing, 2017).

71 Kurt Müller and Gernot Peikert, 'Die Rolle der Glocken im Bauernkrieg 1524/2', in Hegau-Geschichtsverein, *Kriege, Krisen, Friedenszeiten im Hegau, Jahrbuch* (Hegau-Geschichtsverein e.V. Singen/Hohentwiel, 2014), pp. 49–64.

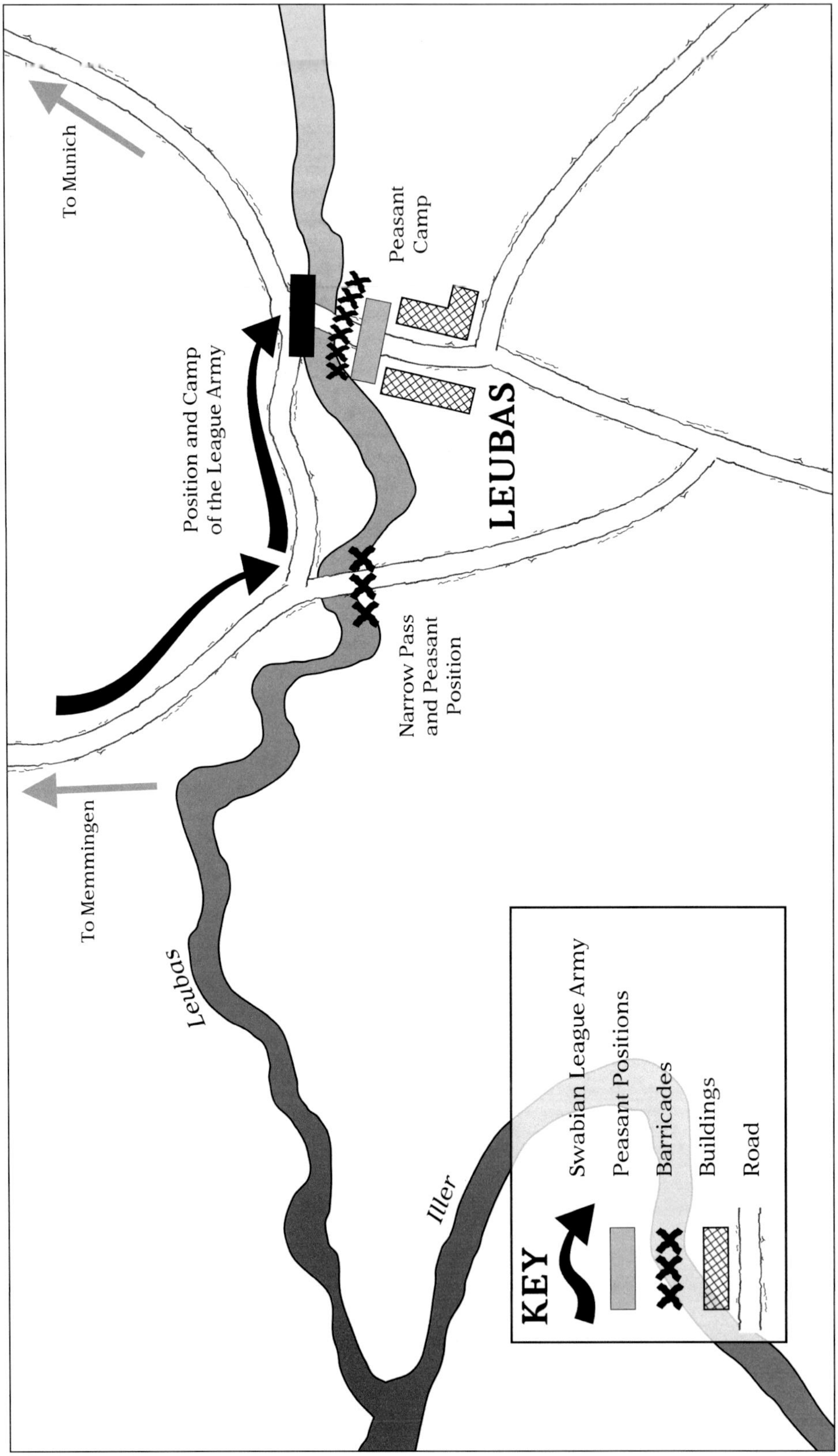

Map 8. The Battle of Leubas, 13 July 1525.

horsemen with body armour.[72] At some point his army would be reinforced by a further 3,000 men under the command of Georg von Frundsberg, who had been commissioned by the League to deal with the rebellion in the diocese of Salzburg.

2.2.16. Georg von Frundsberg (24 September 1473–20 August 1528), has been generally acknowledged as the 'father' of the Landsknechts, having assisted Maximilian 1 in organising the army which was to serve the Holy Roman Empire. He was absent for most of the League campaigns against the Duke of Württemberg, the peasants having been given the command of the German contingents in northern Italy. Following his victory at Pavia he returned to his castle at Mindelheim briefly before recruiting a force to link up with Georg von Waldburg at Leubas in June 1525. His last commission as League supreme commander was against the Austrian peasants who were besieging the fortress of Salzburg in late summer of that year. (Woodcut: Hans Döring 1546, based on a portrait by Christoph Amberger)

Leubas

The forced march took its toll and his army laid up for five days at Wattenweiler. The chronicler Nikolaus Thoman details the carnage wreaked by an obviously starving army of soldiers who plundered everything from livestock to the locals' possessions, 'save the summer and winter fruits'.[73] Jos von Laubenberg, commander of the *Rennfahne*, gained local notoriety after his men burnt down churches deemed to be reformist, and laid waste to farmsteads in the villages of Herrenstetten, Obereichen, and Unter – and Oberdettingen. Within a radius of 20 km of Memmingen – an area consisting of villages with populations varying between 100 and 500, and 20–100 farms – was being devastated by a rampaging behemoth of an army train which because of its length must have appeared never-ending. The upshot served only to drive the peasants who fled their homes further south to join the band which was assembling at Leubas.

The League council had planned for the Truchsess to link up with Georg von Frundsberg at Woringen near Memmingen before heading for the Allgäu but this had not been possible. The League informed Frundsberg of Waldburg's planned route and in the same letter authorised him to recruit and muster troops on their behalf. Frundsberg, having recently returned to his residence at Mindelheim following his successes at Pavia, had not been in a position to recruit the desired number of infantrymen without giving his men their first month's pay. Recruitment was fairly successful by all accounts although the Allgäu peasants too were eagerly recruiting mercenaries on the open market, and had invoked the practice of calling for a doubling up of the militia – part of the protocol for defending the territory.[74] Some 20,000 men were estimated to be gathering at the peasant camp in Obergünzburg. Frundsberg's reputation was probably responsible for the initial roll of 2,000 men, many of whom assembled in Mindelheim. In addition to these contingents, Frundsberg was expecting a troop of *Stradiots* provided by Ludwig of Bavaria. On 7 July he despatched a unit of horse and foot to take delivery of two light field artillery pieces and a supply of 500 pikes from

72 Blickle, p. 273.

73 Nicolaus Thoman, *Weißenhorner Historie* (Stuttgart: Anton H. Konrad Verlag, 1969).

74 R. Baumann, *Georg von Frundsberg: Vater der Landsknechte* (Munich: Süddeutscher Verlag, 1984), p. 236.

Augsburg. He took charge of the muster which was held on 9 July,[75] the same day that the Truchsess was able to get his army moving again from Wattenweiler.

On 12 July Waldburg's army encountered a 3,000-strong band of peasants at Schrattenbach who somewhat late in the day were themselves heading for the rebel camp. He immediately ordered a troop of 200 horse to attack them. A skirmish ensued in which the peasants stood their ground, prompting the League horse to retreat since the main column of foot was still a day's march away.

The following morning on 13 July, thc League army approached Leubas. Leubas had been chosen by the peasants because the terrain provided a great advantage. The village stood in a narrow valley of a tributary of the River Iller by the same name. To the east stood a wood, a pond, and a marshy meadow; to the west, movement was compromised by the course of the River Iller. Leubas had also been a symbolic centre of resistance to the Prince-Abbot of Kempten where various peasant meetings had previously taken place. For the Truchsess this had to be a decisive engagement which would finally break the movement in southern Germany. However, the advantageous position enjoyed by the peasants forced him to take up position on the opposite bank of the river.

There were a few light skirmishes on the 13th but the day was marked by an unprecedented cannonade from both sides.[76] This bought some time for the Truchsess, whose men needed to rest. In a letter to Ulrich Artzt, the Truchsess boasted that the cannonade had only resulted in the deaths of a handful of his men against the 300–400 peasants who had been killed by this action. It is claimed that some 30 hundredweight of gunpowder was consumed, and that a number of cannon barrels had exploded during the action.[77] During the following night both sides undertook special operations. The Truchsess ordered a small team of men to penetrate the peasant camp; some banners were stolen, random fires started, and three cannon pushed down the slope. In addition his men destroyed some of the fascine defences. These men were paid between four and 10 guilders extra for their night's work.[78]

For their part the peasants arranged for a spy by the name of Jakob Lod – a wayfarer from Strasbourg – to infiltrate the League camp for the princely sum of one guilder. Arousing little suspicion, particularly since he had served under Georg von Frundsberg at Pavia, he was tasked with determining and reporting back the size of the League army to Paul Probst, the commander of the Leubas band. Registering with the Nuremberg company, he estimated the number to be 11,000 men, and was sent back into the camp to scout the precise whereabouts of the supreme commander's tent so that the peasants

75 *Ibid.*, pp. 232–3.

76 Blickle, p. 276.

77 Artzt, Report to the Augsburger Council, dated 23 July 1525, op. cit., p. 69.

78 Blickle, p. 277.

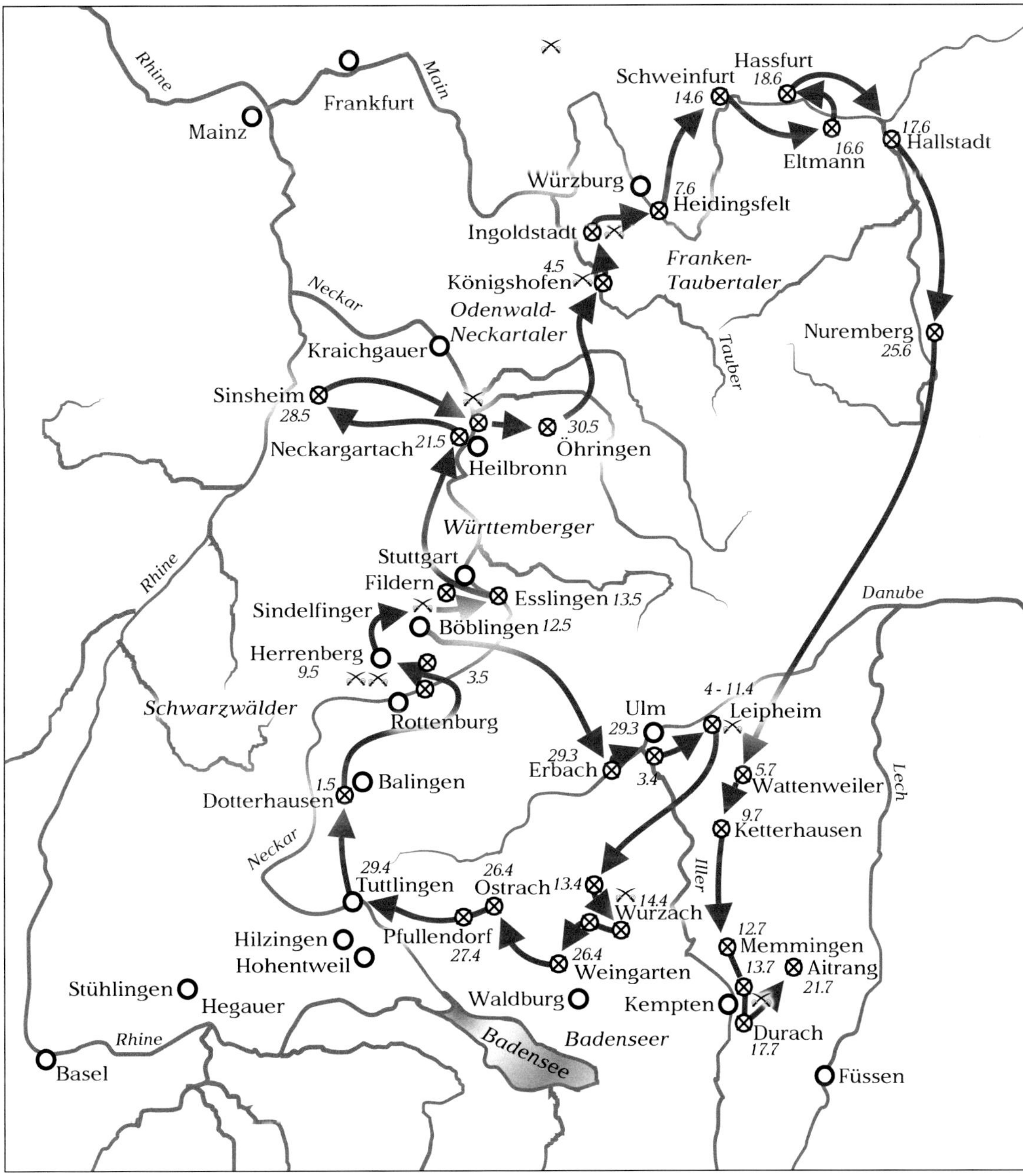

Map 9. The League's campaign trail against the peasants of Upper Swabia, Franconia and the Allgäu.

would be able to train their cannon on this target. However, Lod was prevented from returning by a renewed sortie by the League light horse.[79]

On the morning of the 14th the peasants divided their band into three troops – the aim being to tease the Truchsess into opening and thereby exposing his ranks to a pincer movement. However, the League's *Gewalthaufen* stood firm while several salvos from their falconets damaged the front ranks of the peasants who also had to contend with skirmishing from von Waldburg's light horse. The Truchsess succeeded in forcing the peasants to regroup back in their camp. During the day both sides received reinforcements. The peasants were boosted by the arrival of 2,000 fresh men from the southern Allgäu. On the evening of the 14th, the League army was reinforced by the arrival of Georg von Frundsberg with some eight companies of foot. A frontal assault on the rebel position, given the presence of seasoned Landsknechts in the ranks under the command of experienced commander Walter Bach, would be a highly risky undertaking. Tactics now had to be decided. The League council of war members who essentially followed the army now had to ride from Memmingen to Kempten to consult with the two commanders.

However, as dawn broke on 15 July there was no enemy to be seen. The peasants had evacuated their camp leaving 19 field artillery pieces behind. Contemporary accounts appear to confirm that Walter Bach the peasant commander had been first to withdraw with his band, taking the rest of the peasant army with him.[80] These events were hard to comprehend given the superiority in numbers of the peasant bands which various accounts testify.[81] One theory suggests that Bach was bribed by the League commanders,[82] the task being facilitated by the fact that numbers of Landsknechts in the Allgäu band, including Bach, had fought with Frundsberg in Italy.[83] The chronicler of the Truchsess paints a different picture, however, of a number of spies being sent into the peasant camp who reported that the cannonade on the previous day had, in fact, exhausted all their gunpowder.[84]

A number of peasants billeted in Leubas itself slept through the retreat and were rounded up by units from the League army the following morning, and the town razed to the ground. The Truchsess was keen to pursue the fleeing peasants. Sections of the Allgäu band had withdrawn to the Kohlenberg, a hill near Markt Sulzberg. The hill was soon encircled and the surrounding villages set on fire to demoralise the rebels, whose supplies were quickly running out. The Truchsess had become the scourge of the peasants even to the extent that appointed members of the League council of war Gordian Seuter (Kempten), Hans Freiburger (Überlingen) and Bernhard Goler (Palatine) had unanimously called for a halt to the devastation which von Waldburg was wreaking on the countryside. However, this fell on deaf ears.[85]

79 Baumann, pp. 142–5.
80 Trauchburg, p. 192.
81 Blickle, p. 278.
82 Quoted in Trauchburg, op. cit.
83 *Ibid.*
84 Schreiber, in Baumann, 1876, p. 602.
85 Scribe of Truchsess 603, quoted in Blickle, p. 282.

Box 4 The Confession of Jacob Lod of Strasbourg[86]

In 1526 Jacob Lod appeared before a court in Ravensburg, and apparently without any duress gave up a confession which sheds light on the type of vagabond life which some men led who dropped in and out of mercenary activity at this time.

Born in Strasbourg, Lod grew up with little parental support, leaving his village in the Alsace at the age of 13 having recalled only seeing his mother twice. His confession covered the four years previous to his conviction. We pick him up in 1522 as a vagabond in northern Swabia, dropping in on church festivals and the horse market in Nördlingen, pickpocketing three Batzen in a purse. A knapsack belonging to a tradesman earned him a further three florins while a purloined spice rack brought in a further two guilders. Finally he stole a horse which he was able to sell for three florins.

Moving back to the Alsace, he visited his mother and fell in with two other ruffians – Bat von Rufach and Hanns von Rappotsweiler – both notorious waylayers and murderers. All three made their way to Swabia, thieving two horses in the night which they sold on in the Imperial city of Bopfingen. Rustling became a speciality with the theft of a further horse in Ulm and a cow in Urach.

Following the theft of goods from an inn in Urach, the area became unsafe and they switched their attention to the Allgäu, where as Jacob's Pilgrims they sang and begged their way through the villages in the diocese of Kempten. However, this was not as lucrative as the highway robbery they could engage in on the road to Memmingen. At Isney they attacked a butcher's boy who had little chance against the three of them. They were soon discovered and pursued. While they sat and played cards for the victim's clothes and three florins the body was seen, and they realised they would have to disappear – this time to Switzerland.

In the Inn valley they joined a band of 20 robbers and in the days that followed they drank and gambled and waited for their prey. Three consecutive ambushes yielded considerable booty – a merchant from Trient gave up 500 florins – but they only each received five Batzen for their endeavours. Jacob Lod left then for Sterzing across the Brenner pass and hired himself out to a farmer, but this only lasted three weeks before he rode away on a horse stolen from his employer which he sold in Schwaz. By the end of 1522 he found himself once again in the Allgäu. Hooking up with two other vagabonds they waylaid two pilgrims on their way to Rome, killing them and dividing up the spoils. The next two years were spent begging and stealing – targeting isolated farmsteads. Once again he fell in with two cronies but their thieving led to a fight over the spoils and he ended up killing both.

86 Source: Baumann, pp. 141–145. Loose translation by the author.

During these two years he also attempted to put down roots – in Rammingen near Mindelheim he married, and then a short while after did the same again in Ottobeuren thus committing bigamy, which brought him before the court in Ravensburg. On the 29 September 1524 he robbed and murdered a woman in a wood near Nesselwang and Kempten and as the authorities began to close in he decided to offer his services as a Landsknecht as the recruiting sergeants passed through in search of men for the campaign against Francis I in Northern Italy.

Under the command of Georg von Frundsberg he survived the Battle of Pavia fought on 24 February 1525. Yet immediately after the battle the urge to thieve raged again, and from the plunder gained in the game enclosure at Pavia he stole four pikes and two swords from his fellow travellers, selling them on in the camp market for one and a half florins.

A few days after the victory at Pavia, while many Landsknechts returned back to southern Germany either to serve in the pay of the princes or to side with their peasant brethren, Lod was to be found tramping around and pickpocketing in the yearly markets in Memmingen and Lauingen.

In the summer of 1525 he became a soldier for the second time – this time as a member of the rebel Allgäu band under the command of Paulin Probst. When the Truchsess of Waldburg arrived with the army of the Swabian League and laid siege to the town of Leubas near Kempten, Probst paid Lod a florin and promised him more if he would enter the League camp as a spy. Lod joined the Nuremberg company, pocketing a second florin for his services to the League. Having assessed the strength of the League army he returned to the rebel camp where he was duly paid by Probst and pressed him to undertake a second mission. This time he was to determine the precise location of Waldburg's tent so that the peasants could train their artillery on that position, the aim being to kill the supreme commander. However, Lod was prevented from carrying out the second mission as an attack by the League horse prevented the peasants from taking up a new position.

The defeat of the peasants in the Allgäu prompted Lod to go underground for a period. A few days before Whitsuntide Lod was enlisted by a small band of nine peasants to undertake guerrilla action in Waldburg territory, doing as much fire damage to the Truchsess property as possible. He was provided with powder, slow match and flint and given the sign through which he would recognise his targets. He engaged in fire-raising around Ravensburg where he was finally arrested and handed over to the authorities in Ravensburg where he was tried, convicted and executed on the wheel.

Villages and farms continued to be razed to the ground. Some 3,000 peasants finally surrendered at Sulzberg and were forced to give up their arms and armour, plead for mercy and reaffirm their support for the existing order. One hundred and twelve men were picked out as the officers and ensigns. They would be executed. The remainder were given white staves and ordered to return to their homes – a treacherous journey wherever they were likely to run into Landsknechts in the pay of the League.[87]

The capitulation of the Allgäu band was completed when a further 8,000 peasants surrendered before the Truchsess in Durach. The League was at pains to ensure that von Frundsberg and von Waldburg kept the army together at Durach, but the situation was very fluid with despatches arriving on a daily basis and the wilful extermination of peasants wherever they were found. The humanist polemicist Johannes Chochläus estimated that the Swabian League campaign was responsible for the deaths of some 100,000 souls – an exaggerated figure in the same way that the authorities underestimated the numbers of their losses.[88] The crushing of the rebellion in the Allgäu now needed to be managed and monies extorted from the remaining villages and towns which had not been razed.

On 24 June the League ordered both commanders to retake and punish the municipality of Füssen for failing to recognise the authority of the Bishop of Augsburg and to order them to once again pledge their allegiance to the prelate. This placed them in a difficult position since Füssen had become a protectorate of Archduke Ferdinand as a defensive measure against the peasants. To carry out their orders would have been tantamount to an act of aggression against the Archduke. Moreover, the Austrian horse and foot in their ranks would not have complied. Frundsberg categorically refused to comply with the order. The Truchsess entered the town on a diplomatic rather than military mission, with a troop of 70 men, and was able to return the citizens to the yoke of the Bishop on condition they would go unpunished.

While the Truchsess was engaged in these negotiations the League councillors in Kempten were taking the decision to dissolve the army, and when he returned to the camp at Aitrang near Durach, he discovered that with the exception of the Austrian contingents, his army had dispersed. This must have been demoralising and insulting for the supreme commander who had led his men for six months through an intensive campaign. The excuse given by the League council was that they wanted to save a month's pay.[89]

There was a postscript to this rather ignominious end to von Waldburg's campaign. He submitted a claim to the League for a share of the funds extorted from the peasants. He invoiced the League for one tenth of all the monies extorted during the campaign – estimated by his scribe to be at least 3,000 villages. This was by all accounts a huge amount. After several months of negotiation, the League finally handed over a sum of 5,000 florins – a fifth of what it has been estimated he had personally spent in financing the

87 *Ibid.*, p. 283.
88 Ambrosius Geyer, quoted in Blickle, p. 284.
89 *Ibid.*, p. 287.

campaign.[90] In November he received a letter of commendation from the Emperor Charles V who gave due recognition of his services to the Holy Roman Empire. In the autumn of 1525 he succeeded his cousin Wilhelm as governor of Württemberg, personally receiving the hereditary title of Imperial Steward (*Reichserbtruchsess*) from Charles V on 27 July 1526 at his court in Toledo.

In the meantime, the League still had to keep the peace in its territories and military intervention was still required in the Prince-Bishopric of Salzburg and in the Tyrol, an estate of the Holy Roman Empire which is the northern part of Western Austria today. The Catholic prince-bishop, Matthäus Lang von Wellenburg, had reacted brutally to the spread of Anabaptist and Lutheran preachings in his territory, executing more than 40 Anabaptist preachers and imposing restrictions on the citizens in his see. When two young peasant men were executed for renouncing their Catholic faith this proved to be the final straw, and on 8 May the Archbishop was faced with an uprising of peasants and artisans in his territory, forcing him to seek refuge in the fortress of Salzburg where the rebels laid siege for some 14 weeks. For a period, the rebels were in control of Salzburg as well as parts of Carinthia, Carniola and Upper Austria. On 3 July 1525, the Styrians joined the rebellion and at Schladming dealt a blow to the authorities, capturing their commander and putting to death all of his non-German speaking mercenaries (Croatians and Bohemians). The Prince-Archbishopric which had joined the League in 1512 called for assistance, and Georg von Frundsberg, with the support of Duke Ludwig of Bavaria, was tasked with lifting the siege.

The League army arrived before the gates of Salzburg on 16 August and immediately set about deploying their ordnance to fire on the rebel earthworks, from where their artillery had been trained on the city fortress. There were daily artillery exchanges between the League and rebel guns. Michael Gruber – the rebel leader – was desperate for reinforcements and sent word for help. Duke Ludwig and von Frundsberg knew that a full-scale bombardment and assault would be required and notified the rebel leadership of these plans in an attempt to broker a peace deal. Their threat was successful, and on 31 August a peace treaty was signed, but not before Georg von Frundsberg had extracted a sum of 14,000 florins to pay off his men.[91]

Although an amnesty was agreed on release of the Prince-Archbishop and a promise to review the rebels' grievances, the Archbishop was soon embarking on a campaign to punish the rebels under Michael Gaismair, who had delivered a blow against the authorities at Schladming. At the end of September Frundsberg travelled to Innsbruck from where he took part in the regional assembly at Bozen as the supreme commander of the Tyrol.[92] In December he returned to his castle at Mindelheim. This marked the end of

90 *Ibid.*, pp. 289–90.
91 Karl Köchl, 'Die Bauernkriege im Erzstifte Salzburg in den Jahren 1525 und 1526', in *Mitteilungen der Gesellschaft für Salzburger Landeskunde* (MGSLK) 47 1907, pp. 57–63.
92 Reinhard Baumann, *Anna von Lodron, ein adeliges Frauenleben in der Reformationszeit* (Innsbruck: Universitätsverlag Wagner, 2015), p. 50.

2.2.17. Fortress of Hohensalzburg. The complex acquired the appearance we recognise today under Archbishop Leonhard von Keutschach in 1500. The original purpose of the fortress was to protect the principality, and Archbishop Matthäus Lang sought refuge there from his subjects for several months during 1525. (Courtesy: Ra Boe)

Swabian League military activity during 1525. From the end of the year to the end of the decade much of the ensuing military debate within the League concerned the question of reparations and claims by members for financial assistance to meet debts incurred in raising troops which they had expected the League to cover. For example there was the complaint by Margrave Casimir Brandenburg concerning the failure of the League to provide troop contingents he had requested, which resulted in him having to bear the cost of defeating the peasants at Ostheim.[93] Further demands for raising contingents emerged as disturbances continued in the Upper Rhineland and in Franconia (Rothenburg).[94] The rapid action force contingents were renewed and increased in 1528 to 946 horse and 5,642 foot.[95]

By 1530 the League was in decline. In the ensuing period after the Peasants' War, religious tensions within the membership of the League gradually caused its demise. The Imperial cities had largely become Protestant, whereas the feudal territories belonging to the nobility clung to the Catholic faith. Following the Battle of Lauffen in 1534 Duke Ulrich was once again restored as ruler of Württemberg and the Duchy converted to Protestantism in the same year. Württemberg finally broke away to join the Schmalkaldic League, a military alliance established in 1531 by Philip I, Landgrave of Hesse, and John Frederick I, Elector of Saxony, the two most powerful Protestant rulers in the Holy Roman Empire at the time. The Swabian League was formally wound up on 2 February 1534, much of its business being taken over by the Swabian Circle. There were two futile attempts to renew it, in 1535 by the Bavarian chancellor, Eck, and in 1547 by Charles V.

93 Klüpfel, pp. 302–3.

94 *Ibid.*, 299.

95 *Ibid.*, 331–2.

Afterword

From the appointment of Georg von Waldburg as the supreme commander on 2 February, the League campaigns lasted 168 days, some five and a half months. The army covered some 1,866 kilometres (see maps), and according to the diaries of the Truchsess administered some form of justice to 3,000 villages. The troop contingents at full strength, that is 6,276 foot and 1,967 horse (as at Leipheim), remained fairly constant during this period, although they were boosted by the arrival of Frundsberg's force at Leubas with an extra 3,000 men. Peasant numbers fluctuated but in general it can be said that they outnumbered the League troops. This numerical advantage was, however, no match for the tactical and logistical superiority of von Waldburg's army. Despite signs of a decline in the effectiveness of the mounted knight, as seen in the battles of the Italian Wars, the dominance of the League in all its military engagements against the peasants owed much to the Truchsess's deployment of light horse in particular. To some extent this was determined by the supreme commander's own chivalrous intent. A further explanation lies in the fact that the light horse was first to arrive at the site of battle, and in the absence of mounted opposition could cut a swathe through the ranks of peasant foot. We must also consider the unreliability of sections of the League infantry, the bulk of which were recruited from the cities and the prelates – the former having shifting allegiances to the peasant cause.

There is an overwhelming sense from various accounts of the campaign that discipline within the League ranks was fragile – with much hinging on the mood of the infantry whose commitment to the cause was indeed faltering, and whose loyalty could only be bought off with the promise of a victory bonus or a share in the spoils of war. Logistically, the League army must have appeared like a behemoth trundling through the countryside with its vast supply and baggage train sparing only those homesteads capable of paying a fire avoidance tax, but ruthlessly dealing with anyone remotely involved in the organisation of the uprising. A conservative estimate of peasant casualties notes a figure of 20,750 against an unrealistic 100 losses on the part of the League.[1] Given the absence of alternative accounts by supporters of the peasant cause, these figures have to be approached with some caution.

1 Blickle, pp. 294–5.

Appendix I

Extracts from the Ochsenfurter Field Ordinances 24–27 April 1525

This is one of the few examples remaining of a field ordinance (*Feldordnung*) in which the command structure of the army would be laid down. This example was drawn up by the Franconian peasants and is clearly modified but based on a typical letter of articles of the day.

9. … it is considered that the supreme commander shall have four aides appointed alongside him, and the lieutenant two, to serve alongside them day and night, and loyally to follow their requests and orders.

10. The supreme commander [*Oberster Befehlshaber*] and the lieutenant [*Leutinger*] shall have their lodgings and tents near the cannon, so that they can be found by day or night in case of need.

…

13. A captain is to be elected[1] by each troop, to whom those in the troop may reveal their needs and grievances. Afterwards, the same captains shall present these grievances to the supreme commander in the presence of the appointed captains and councillors, which will be discussed by them, and so all disorder and trouble will be kept in check.

14. From each company comprising around five hundred men, one man shall be elected[2] as colour-sergeant. And the elected colour-sergeant shall be obliged, as is fitting, to exercise his office truly and honourably, as far as his honour and bodily power permit.

1 League captains would have been appointed.

2 Again, this officer would have been an appointee.

15. A sheriff [*Schultheiss*] is to be appointed ..., and he is to administer justice each day, as often as the need arises, alongside the appointed assessors or jurors who have been or may in future be appointed, and to punish the evil and advance and protect justice. And in this he shall let himself be influenced by no bribes, fees, friendships, or enmities, but keep before his eyes ... only God and his justice. The sheriff shall have two aides appointed to assist him.

16. One man is to be appointed ... as provost-marshal [*Profoss*] . He shall exercise his office in the following manner. First, whenever camp is pitched, he shall immediately erect a gallows for the punishment of the wicked ... He shall arrest all evildoers and transgressors and hold them in secure custody, and afterwards present the misdeeds of each to the captains and councillors. Whatever orders are sent to the provost-marshal after the presentation and assessment of the accused, he is to implement. The provost-marshal shall have no power of his own to do violence to or to levy anyone, ... but only on the orders, and by the will and knowledge of the supreme commander and the appointed councillors. He shall on his oath hand over the confiscated or acquired goods or money to the captains and councillors, or whoever else has so entrusted him, and not retain them in his power.

17. The provost-marshal shall also, as soon as camp is pitched, assess all the provisions brought into the camp according to fair prices, whether it be bread, wine, meat, or other victual. If corn, wheat, or oats are brought in, he shall also price them fairly and shall take a shilling from each wagon and three pence from a cart as his fee ...

18. For the office of master of artillery [*Oberster Zeugmeister*], armourer, and master of the arsenal, ... shall be in sole command of the cannon and keep it in good order and security ...

19. A master of the wagonfort [*Wagenburgmeister*] is to be appointed, and his command is that when camp is struck and moves off, the wagons are to move off and proceed according to his orders. However he orders them to proceed, they shall keep that order, and the carts are not be mixed in among the wagons.

20. The office of master of the watch shall have four appointed to it, who are to use their true diligence so that when camp is pitched, watch will be kept as necessary.

21. Four sergeants shall be appointed ... to make a battle-order ...

22. Then there shall be appointed a sergeant for each troop, to march alongside the ranks, and whoever shall fall out of the ranks he shall

drive back into them. On the march everyone is to remain where he has been ordered and not leave the ranks, on pain of punishment.

23. Two quartermasters are to be elected to supervise the kitchens and cellars, so that they can be kept in good and uniform order.

24. A master of the spoils is to be appointed in each company, so that booty will be distributed equally and no one receive more or less advantage than another.

25. A paymaster shall be appointed and everyone shall pay him for provisions consumed and the like.

Source: Scott and Scribner (edited by the present author).

Appendix II

Regimental Rates of Pay in Florins (as laid down at the Imperial Diet of Constance 1507)

Rank	**Rate × 4**	**Pay @ × 4**
Supreme Commander	100	400
Lieutenant	25	100
Chaplain	3	12
Scribe	6	24
Master of the Watch	10	40
Commissary	10	40
Surgeon (*Feldscherer*)	10	40
Field medic	10	40
Drummer	2	8
Fifer	2	8
Translator	2	8
Cook	2	8
Carter	1	4
Bodyguard/Aide de Camp	1	4
Commander of the Train (*Hurenweibel*)	3	12

Appendix III

Company Rates of Pay in Florins (as laid down at the Imperial Diet of Constance 1507)

Rank	Rate × 4	Pay @ × 4
Captain (x 10)	10	400
Lieutenant	5	200
Standard Bearer	5	200
Chaplains	2	80
Sergeants	3	120
Squad leaders	1	40
Fourier	1	40
Corporals	1	80
Drummers	1	80
Aides-de-camp	1	80
Translators	1	40
Captain's boy	1	40
Ensign's boy	1	40
Captain's cook	1	40
Mounted body guard	1	40
Staff for military justice		236

Appendix IV

The Austrian (Habsburg) Contingent of horse in the League Army on the Eve of the Battle of Leipheim (3 April) 1525 (Brackets indicate accompanying men)

Graf Ludwig von Lupfen (9), Graf Friedrich von Fürstenberg (12), Graf Ulrich von Helfenstein (8), Herr Hans Walther von Laubenberg (5), Herr Frowein von Hutten (12), Herr Wolf von Homburg (6), Herr Georg von Rechberg (7), Konrad von Reischach (3), Heinrich Marschalk (8), Hans Adam vom Stain (6), Georg Heuslin (4), Wilhelm Marschal (5), Philipp von Landau (4), Hans Fuchs (5), Markward von Schwendi (3), Hans von Erolzheim (5), Georg von Endingen (5), Kaspar von Neustetten (1), Jörg von Laubenberg (5), Joachim Marschalk (5), Hans Ulrich Sürg (5), Frick Humpiss (4), Georg Weichsner (16), Georg Handtzeller (3), Jakob von Ramsberg (4), Bastian Schenk (5), Eberhard von Reischach (3), Hans Jakob Dentzel (4), Hans Koch (2), Lorenz Wunderlich (1), Paul Dietrich von Denken (1), Bernhard Segk (1), Hans Müller (1), Wilhelm Schwarzmann (1), Hans Jäger (1), Wolf Sigmund von Buch (1), Klaus von Schaumberg (3), Wendel zum Weier (4), Bat von Pfirt (3), Paul Stör (6), Ludwig Wolf von Renchen (2), Kaspar von Milheim (4), Wolf Waldner (4), Humprecht von Wessenburg (3), Sigmund von Truttenberg (2), Peter von Brinkhofen (2), Kaspar Arnolt (2), Lienhart Ainspennig Antoni Tresch (1), Wolf Dietrich von Homburg (5), Wolf von Stainen (4), Hans von Ehingen (4), Bastian von Ehingen (6), Bastian von Gültlingen (5), Christran Truchsäss (4), Bernhard von Liebenstein (2), Ludwig von Morstein (3), Hans von Riexingen (3), Marx von Schornstetten (2), Hans von Karpfen (2), Reichwein (2), Hans von Au (2), Hans von Lenberg (1), Hereinsen (1), Wolf Thaub (1), Jäcklin von Urach (1), Jörg Hildt (1), Theus (1), Hans von Stamen (1), Simon Altpiesser (1), Franz Schertlin (2), Wolf Märk (1), Georg Karter (1), Lang Georg (1), Christoff (1), Auberlin (1), Utz Aff (1), Ruffer

Henßlin (1), Kilian von Böblingen (1), Eberhard von Frauenberg von wegen meines gn. Hn. Markgrafen (30), Gundelfingen (5), Stauffer (11), Eberhard von Hernegk Schnabel (1), Ott von Gemmingen (8), Bartholme Motz (2), Gordian von der Schör (2), Renhardt Gailing (3), Konrad von Reckenbach (4), Walter von Habsberg (7), Adam Herkum (3), Hans Wolf von Habsberg (3), Lienhard Prenner (5), Rudolf Ebner (3), Seggendorfer (2), Philipp Höß (1), Martin Walshammer (2), Lienhard Hag (1), Fahrig (1), Kupferlin (1), Christoph von Habsberg Otingen (7), Sigmund Tregenreiter (1), Hipsch Georg (1), Schreiber von Buchau (1), Hans Maug (1), Georg Streitfelder (1), Christoph Reich (1), Georg von Rot (4), Trutzkirchen (6), Wilhelm von Königsegg Blesi Taler (1)

Source: Blickle, pp. 296–7.

Colour Plate Commentaries

Plate 1

Command Group of the Swabian League army. Preceded by a unit of light horse (*Rennfahne*) the commanders rode at the head of the main column. Figure **A** shows Georg Truchsess von Waldburg clad in 'Maximilian' armour. Immediately to his rear are his three unit commanders: **B** – Michael Ott von Echterdingen (artillery), **C** – Wilhelm von Fürstenberg (infantry), and **D** – Frowen von Hutten (horse). With the development of coats of arms during the Middle Ages it soon became possible for commanders to recognise their units of men both through the banner, the caparison, the shield and the surcoat. As warfare progressed in the early modern era and infantry grew in prominence, shields and surcoats began to disappear, knights being recognised by their standards and coloured plumage. Heraldry on banners and standards became significant markers for troop movements and had to be defended at all costs as a matter of honour. Each knight would have had their own ensign. To their rear from left to right are the banners of the houses of **E** -Waldburg, **F** – Fürstenberg, and **G** – Hutten. To the right at the rear, figure **H** is Hans Lutz, the League army herald.

They are clad in the dominant two styles of armour at this time – the ridged German design and the smooth Italian 'Milanese' armour. Armour production in the German-speaking countries centred on several hubs: the Imperial cities of Augsburg, Basel (Swiss after 1501), Landshut, and Nuremberg, as well as the court workshop of the Holy Roman Emperors in Innsbruck. In Augsburg, the Helmschmied family, with its most prominent members Lorenz (*c.* 1445–1516), Kolman (1471–1532), and Desiderius (1513–1579) worked for the Archdukes of Austria and Tyrol, as well as the Holy Roman Emperor. The characteristic parallel decorative ridges and grooves known as 'fluting' could cover virtually the entire suit of armour (usually with the exception of the greaves). Such 'fluted armour', because of its development roughly coinciding with the reign of Emperor Maximilian I (1493–1519), is commonly referred to as 'Maximilian' style.

The command group are depicted in contemporary images with fully armoured horses (see image 2.2.5 in the main text). By the mid fifteenth century, metal plates and leather were the dominant materials for all elements of horse armour, and a 'full bard' now comprised a shaffron, closed neck defence (crinet), chest protection (peytral), panels for the sides (flanchards), and a rump defence (crupper). Matching sets of armour for horse and rider, including saddles covered with steel plates, were a particular speciality of Lorenz Helmschmid (1445–1516) the Augsburg armourer. Edges could be scalloped and pierced with various patterns, and surfaces were embossed with ridges and grooves. Plate armour could be further decorated with appliqués of copper alloy as well as bluing, gilding, and etching, although this was more likely to be found in ceremonial pieces. The effectiveness of such armour was a matter of debate, with none other than Niccolo Machiavelli commenting that German heavy horse:

> … in combat with Italian or French men-at-arms they would not prevail – not because of their inability as such but because their horse is poorly armoured – their saddles too small and poorly reinforced causing the knights to be easily thrown to the ground at the slightest blow.[1]

Plate 2

Foot contingents from the cities in particular would also be recognisable by the municipal heraldry borne on their respective banners. A selection of heraldic emblem flags representing some of the principal members of the Swabian League is shown here. This plate shows the banners of **A** – Augsburg, **B** – Bamberg, **C** – Bavaria, and **D** – Biberach. The images depicted here from the heraldic work of Jakob Köbel completed in 1545 when costume was beginning to undergo a change towards the *Pluderhose* style. The banners themselves show quite large (if not exaggerated) folds of fabric. Note how the artist here has generally continued the colour scheme of the banner in the costume of the flagbearer in *mi parti* style.

Plate 3

Shows the banners **A** –Brandenburg, **B** – Habsburg, **C** – Landshut and **D** – Mainz.

The standard bearers were dressed as befitted their rank. Landsknechts were noted for their garish costume which exaggerated the slashing and folds of the day. The extent of embellishment must, however, be taken with a degree of caution. Some of the more flamboyant woodcut depictions of individuals were commissions and the name of the subject appeared on the print with a piece of verse.[2] We do not know whether certain embellishments were added for effect on request when the subject was more modestly attired.

---

1 Niccolo Machiavelli, 'The political situation in Germany at the beginning of the 16th century', in *Collected Works Vol. 2* (Munich 1925), p. 214, quoted in Hoyer, p. 30.

2 G.A. Johann, B. Enkevoerth, J. von Falke, and M. McNealy (eds), *Landsknecht Woodcuts: Kriegsvölker im Zeitalter der Landsknechte* (Quakenbrück: Nadel und Faden Press, 2013).

Most definitely the rigours of campaign and battle would have compromised the extent of experimentation with this style.

Plate 4

These coloured drawings are from a whole series cataloguing the Imperial arsenal inventory at Innsbruck and painted by Bartholomaeus Freysleben. Plate **A** shows a falconet (*Falkonett*) usually pulled by a single horse. **B** depicts a slightly larger and longer-barrelled fieldpiece known as a culverin (*Feldschlange*)**.** **C** is a larger demi-cannon (*Kartaune*) used for bombardment). **D** shows a limber (*Protze*) bearing a number of metal struts used to stabilise the carriage during transport. Source: *Zeugbuch Kaiser Maximilians I* (Maximilian's Book of Artillery) – Bayerische Staatsbibliothek München Clm 222, fol. 19r resp. 58r. The whole catalogue is available for viewing online under the identifier BSB Cod.icon. 222 at the Munich DigitalisierungsZentrum.

Plate 5

Detail of costume worn by the lesser nobility at the court of Dukes William and Albrecht William of Bavaria, some of whom would have served in the squadrons of the League light horse. Note how in some cases a frock coat is worn over the armour. This may have been discarded for battle. Source: *Hofkleiderbuch des Herzogs Wilhelm IV. und Albrecht V. 1508–1551*, Bayerische Staatsbibliothek, Munich BSB Cgm 1952, [BSB-Hss Cgm 1952] urn:nbn:de:bvb:12-bsb00016900-2

Plate 6

Swabian League banners: **A** – Memmingen, **B** – Nuremberg, **C** – Palatinate, **D** – Salzburg.

Plate 7

Swabian League Banners**:** **A** – Esslingen , **B** – Würzburg, **C** – Ulm, **D** – Überlingen.

Source: *Wapen des Heyligen Römischen Reichs Teutscher Nation* or *Arms of the German nation of the Holy Roman Empire*. Preface by Jacob Köbel (Frankfurt am Main, 1545). Courtesy: Bayerische Staatsbibliothek München, Cgm [VD16 K 1623].

Plate 8

Coloured drawing **A** is of an artillery train in transit consisting of four columns. Note the pontoons. It was usually left to the cities to provide the wagons for the train and they often carried a pennant fore and aft on the ridge of the wagon canopy bearing the municipal coat of arms, as depicted here. Source: Franz Helm, *Das Buch von den probierten Künsten* 1535, Courtesy University Library Heidelberg <http://digi.ub.uni-heidelberg.de/diglit/cpg128/0425> (accessed 2 July 2018).

Drawing **B** shows a ubiquitous open-sided wagon used for the transport or munitions and equipment in the artillery train. Drawing **C** depicts a covered wagon with optional wicker side panels. Source: Ludwig von Eyb, der Jüngere (1450–1521) Kriegsbuch – UER H62/MS.B 26 BL 275 and 278r. Courtesy: University Library Erlangen-Nürnberg.

Bibliography

Bach, V., 'Markets for Mercenaries: Supplying Armies in Sixteenth-Century Germany', in McWilliams, M. (ed.), *Food & markets: proceedings of the Oxford Symposium on Food and Cookery* 2014 (London: Prospect Books, 2015), pp. 33–45

Barthhold, F.W., *Georg von Frundsberg oder das deutsche Kriegshandwerk zur Zeit der deutschen Reformation* (Hamburg: Friedrich Perthes, 1833), pp. 357–362

Baumann, R., *Georg von Frundsberg: Vater der Landsknechte* (Munich: Süddeutscher Verlag 1984)

Baumann, R., *Landsknechte* (Munich: C.H. Beck Verlag, 1994)

Baumann, R., in Brockling, U., 'Protest und Verweigerung in der Zeit der klassischen Söldnerheere', in *Armeen Und Ihre Deserteure: Vernachlässigte Kapitel einer Militärgeschichte der Neuzeit* (Göttingen: Sammlung Vandenhoeck,1998), pp. 39–44

Baumann, R., 'Böhmische Söldner', in *Historisches Lexikon Bayerns* <http://www.historisches-lexikon-bayerns.de/Lexikon/BöhmischeSöldner> (accessed 13 August 2018)

Belfort Bax, E., *The Peasants' War in Germany 1525–1526* (London: Swan Sonnenschein, 1899)

Blickle, P., *Der Bauernjörg. Feldherr im Bauernkrieg* (Munich: C.H. Beck Verlag, 2015)

Breiding, Dirk H. 'Famous Makers of Arms and Armors and European Centers of Production', in Heilbrunn Timeline of Art History. New York: The Metropolitan Museum of Art, 2000–. <http://www.metmuseum.org/toah/hd/make/hd_make.htm> (October 2002). Accessed 13 October 2018.

Frisch, E. v., *Der 'Salzburger Bauernkrieg' des Egidius Rem in seiner ursprünglichen Fassung von 1525* <http://www.zobodat.at/pdf/MGSL_82_83_0081-0091.pdf> (accessed 9 October 2018)

Hasselbeck, J., *Die Folgen des Deutschen Bauernkriegs im Hochstift Bamberg* (Bamberg: University of Bamberg Press, 2012)

Horst, Carl, 'Der Schwäbische Bund 1488–1534 – Landfrieden und Genossenschaft im Übergang vom Spätmittelalter zur Reformation', Reihe: *Schriften zur südwestdeutschen Landeskunde*, band 24 (Ostfildern: Jan Thorbecke Verlag 2000)

Hoyer, S., *Das Militärwesen im deutschen Bauernkrieg 1524–1526* (Berlin: Deutscher Militärverlag, 1975)

Huber, Barbara, *Im Zeichen der Unruhe: Symbolik bäuerlicher Protestbewegungen im oberdeutschen und eidgenössischen Raum 1400–1700*, PhD Philosophisch-historischen, Faculty of the University of Berne submitted 11. November 2005, pp. 172–178

Johann, G.A., Enkevoerth, B., von Falke, J., and McNealy, M. (eds), *Landsknecht Woodcuts: Kriegsvölker im Zeitalter der Landsknechte* (Quakenbrück: Nadel und Faden Press, 2013)

Klüpfel, K. (ed.), *Urkunden zur Geschichte des Schwäbischen Bundes (1488–1533)* (Stuttgart: Literarischer Verein, 1853).

Köchl, K., *Die Bauernkriege im Erzstift Salzburg in den Jahren 1525 und 1526*. 1814 <https://www.zobodat.at/pdf/MGSL_47_0001-0117.pdf> (accessed 9 October 2018)

Miller, D., *Armies of the German Peasants War 1524–6* (Oxford: Osprey, 2003)

Moxey, K., *Peasants, Warriors and Wives* (Chicago: Chicago Press 1989)

Müller, K. und Peikert, G., 'Die Rolle der Glocken im Bauernkrieg 1524/2', in Hegau-Geschichtsverein, *Kriege, Krisen, Friedenszeiten im Hegau, Jahrbuch* (Hegau-Geschichtsverein e.V. Singen/Hohentwiel 2014). S. 49–64.

Oakeshott, E., *European Weapons and Armour* (Suffolk: Boydell Press, 1980)

Ossan, E., *Zur Geschichte Des Schwäbischen Bundes, Von 1487 Bis 1493* (Charleston: Nabu Press, 2010)

Richards, J., *Landsknecht Soldier* (Oxford: Osprey, 2002)

Scott, T., and Scribner, R. (eds), *The German Peasants' War. A History in Documents* (Amherst: Prometheus Books, 1991)

Rogg, M., 'Landsknechte und Reisläufer: Bilder vom Soldaten: Ein Stand in der Kunst des 16. Jahrhunderts', dissertation, *Krieg in der Geschichte*, band 5 (Paderborn: Verlag Ferdinand Schöningh, 2002)

Vochezer, J., *Geschichte des fürstlichen Hauses Waldburg in Schwaben*, Bd. 2 (Kempten 1900, 422–768)

Vogt, L., *1504 Die Chronik des Georg Schwarzerdt* (Ubstadt-Weiher: Verlag Regionalkultur, 2000). See also <http://www.guenther-gropp.de/images/stories/bretten/HS220Schwarzerdchronik.pdf> (accessed 09 October 2019).

Vogt. W., 'Die Correspondenz des schwäbischen Bundeshauptmanns Ulrich Artzt von Augsburg a. d. J. 1524 und 1525. Ein Beitrag zur Geschichte des Bauernkrieges', in *Zeitschrift des Historischen Vereins für Schwaben*, Jahrgang 6 und 7 (1880), Jg 9 (1882), Jg 10 (1883).